# Get Psyched

# Get Psyched

## Psychology Basics

*Bill Conn*

iUniverse, Inc.
New York Lincoln Shanghai

## Get Psyched
## Psychology Basics

Copyright © 2005 by Bill Conn

iUniverse books may be ordered through booksellers or by contacting:

iUniverse
2021 Pine Lake Road, Suite 100
Lincoln, NE 68512
www.iuniverse.com
1-800-Authors (1-800-288-4677)

ISBN-13: 978-0-595-36869-3 (pbk)
ISBN-13: 978-0-595-67429-9 (cloth)
ISBN-13: 978-0-595-81280-6 (ebk)
ISBN-10: 0-595-36869-7 (pbk)
ISBN-10: 0-595-67429-1 (cloth)
ISBN-10: 0-595-81280-5 (ebk)

Printed in the United States of America

# Contents

# Introduction

This simplified text was developed to give a snapshot overview of some basic concepts in the science of Psychology. This basic aid to instruction and learning will introduce you to Psychology and hopefully whet your appetite to continue your studies in this very interesting field. It is designed to give you some insight into the mind and behavior of the individual human and therefore help you understand the actions of others. If this book in any way helps you through your life's journey than it has done its job.

# Dedication

I would like to dedicate this book to my parents. To my Dad who taught me the lessons of diligence and service to country. And most importantly, to my Mother whose love and encouragement has motivated me throughout my life. Their generation is very aptly called the "greatest generation". We all owe them so much.

# Unit I

## Introduction

# Chapter 1

## Basics of Psychology

**Psychology**—The science that deals with the behavior and thinking of organisms. Derived from the Greek words *Psyche* and *Logos*.

    Psyche—mind or soul

    Logos—study of…

Definition contains 4 important words: *Science, Behavior, Thinking, and Organism.*

    Science—Study that is based on systematically conducted research.

    Behavior—Activities of people or animals that can be observed directly or measured by special techniques (ex. Emotions).

    Thinking—Unobservable activity by which a person or animal reorganizes past experiences through the use of symbols and concepts.

    Organism—Any living person or animal.

Abnormal Psychology—Only one of the many areas of concern for psychologists, sometimes confused as the major study.

Sciences that have contributed greatly to making this a "true" science…

    Physics—Instruments for measuring bodily changes (ex. PET Scan)

    Chemistry—Body's chemistry relates to mood, performance, and personality disturbances (ex. Prozac)

    Biology—Understanding heredity, information about our sense organs, nervous system, glands, and the brain.

(*Note: Still the main focus of this science is mainly *behavior*.)

Anthropology—Study of *cultures*, or ways of life of people in all parts of the world.

Sociology—Study of human *groups* and most closely related science to psychology.

Social Psychology—Concerned with the effects of groups on the individual and with how individuals think about other people.

**History**—Only existed for about a century, with behavior being studied for the first time in the late 1800's.

Stone Age—The thought that spirits inhabited the body. The ancient belief in evil spirits contributing to the mental state of people still exists today in some cultures.

Ancient Egypt—Smaller person called *Ka* lived in the body. The number of "Ka" usually stopped at 7.

Ancient Greece—Behavior was believed to have stemmed from philosophies of the time.

> Plato—Believed the mind and body were two distinct elements.
> Aristotle—Believed that the mind and body were related as one unit.
> Hippocrates—"Father of Medicine", believed that abnormal behavior was caused by disease or a chemical imbalance. Based many of his theories on the *"humors"* of the body (blood, phlegm, black bile, and yellow bile).

Middle Ages—Once again thought that our actions were based on good and evil spirits (ex. Exorcism and Astrology).

1600 and 1700's—In Europe behavior was believed to be related to the biological.

Descartes—First to mention the *"mind-body"* connection, and also how influences the other but neither is controlled by each other.

Phrenology—A false science that is based on the bumps on a person's Head and the "faculties" they control.

Wilhelm Wundt—The science of Psychology was believed to have started when Wundt began his studies at the University of Leipzig in Germany in 1879.

*Wilhelm Wundt*

*Introspection*—How people examine their own thoughts.

*Experimentation*—An essential element of science that he introduced to Psychology.

*Structuralism*—The basic format of Wundt's concept that is based on the "structure" of human consciousness.

William James—A Harvard professor who studied how the mind works and how the human mind "functions" in helping us to adapt to our surroundings—thus came his concept of psychology which is known as *Functionalism.*

*William James*

Sigmund Freud—Came from Vienna, Austria in the late 1800's. His concept of *Psychoanalysis* was based on the idea that human behavior is greatly influenced by the feelings and wishes that are buried deep inside us. Because it is based on making us aware of our unconscious mind he used these three tools:

1. Hypnosis
2. Dream Analysis
3. Free Association

*Sigmund Freud*

The "Behaviorists": Watson, Skinner, and Bandura

John Watson—Believed in the study of observable behavior (surroundings and Personalities). Started in helping us understand the relation that rewards and punishments has in determining our behavior. Believed that there is no such thing as "free will".

*John Broadus Watson*

B.F. Skinner—Probably the best known of the Behaviorists. Expanded Upon Watson's theories and developed many of his own, sometimes Controversial theories. Best known for Reinforcement theories and "shaping".

*B.F. Skinner*

Albert Bandura—Believed that behavior is learned, mostly through observation and imitation (i.e. Models).

*Albert Bandura*

Gestalt Psychology—(German for shape, or form) The use of the five senses to extract information from the environment. "The whole is more important than the sum of its parts".

Cognitive Psychology—Focuses on how we perceive, store, and interpret information. Also studies how thought processes develop over time, and how we draw relations between our thoughts and our feelings.

Existential Psychology—Stresses the importance of "individual choice" in determining human behavior. Contrary to Behaviorists, we do have free will. States that behavior is determined by past events and choices we make.

Humanistic Psychology—Based on how people try to achieve their maximum potential (or Self-Actualization) through health, goals, and self-growth. Believes that humans are the sum of their parts.

(*Note: Most Psychologists of today use an eclectic, or combined approach in their study and treatment of patients.)

Careers that involve the study of Psychology...

Psychiatrists—Have Medical Degrees. Prevention, Diagnosis, and Treatment of disturbances. Can prescribe drugs to patients.

Psychologists—Usually have Ph.D., Doctor of Psychology, or Educational degree at the Masters or Doctorate level.

Degrees:
>   Bachelor Degree—About 4 years. Allows for employment in Personal Administration, Management Training, Sales, Advertising, Government, and Social Services. Titles can have the term Therapist, Teacher, or Nurse after some specific area name.

>   Masters Degree—4 years undergraduate and about 2 additional years. Allows for occupational work with Children (school), Testing, Psychological Clinics, and Teaching (College). Titles can have the term Counselor after the specific area names.

>   Doctoral—4 years of undergrad., and 4-6 years at Graduate and Doctorate Level. Usually has the title of Psychologist after the specific area name and are referred to as Dr. So-and-so. Will probably need to complete a Thesis and go before a Board of Faculty.

Some Career Areas:

*Experimental Psychologist*—Studies the relationship between two or more variables. Deals primarily in experimentation. Works in a laboratory setting with animals mostly, but some human study can also be done with APA approval. Areas of study are mostly in Sensation & Perception, Learning & Remembering, Emotional behavior, and Motivation. Proficiency in Math and Statistics.

*Developmental Psychologist*—(In the past primarily known as a Child Psychologist) Studies the changes in behavior over stages of life, but mostly in children. Patient field goes from infancy to older adult years. Areas that they need to be proficient in are Language, Intellect, Social attachments, Emotions,

Creativity, Physical skills, Thinking, Perception, Retirement, Male and Female roles, and many combined areas of the above.

*Rehabilitation Counselor*—(Goes by other names as well) Works with the handicapped or special needs population. Helps to find them jobs so they can be self-supporting, or schooling to help make that happen. Placement may be based on intelligence or aptitude tests that the Counselor can administer. Works with many outside agencies and corporations, and needs to do continuous checks on their progress.

*Special Education Teacher*—Works with a variety of special-needs students from gifted; to the mentally handicapped; to those with physical, emotional, and learning problems. Occupational considerations are mainstreaming/inclusion and the teaching of life skills.

*Personnel Manager*—Hired by companies and corporations to hire employees, run training programs, give work assignments, consider promotions, evaluate productivity, salary scales, and benefits programs; and deal occasionally in public relations.

*School Psychologist*—Works with Students, Teachers, Administrators, and Parents. Evaluate and administer a variety of evaluative tests. They help students with special needs and also help students and parents deal with conflicts in the educational and home settings.

*Educational Psychologist*—They are normally the ones who teach the teachers on teaching techniques, curriculum, and new learning concepts. Usually hired by Colleges and Universities, they also get highly involved in research.

*Occupational Therapist*—Deal primarily with the physically or mentally disabled in returning them to a hopefully normal day-to-day living environment. Work hand and hand with Dr.'s, Social Workers, Psychologists, and Nurses to teach them skills to return to the work force.

*Marriage/Family Counselor*—Work with couples and families who are having difficulties. They help build stronger relationships or possibly even suggest separations. Have to be available at all hours of the day.

*Guidance Counselor*—Mostly in a school setting; they help students in a number of areas from school situations, parent problems, college selection and scholarships, and future job recommendations.

*Industrial Psychologist*—Deal with "human" problems at work, labor-management problems, productivity strategies, consumer likes & dislikes, and the ergonomics involved with equipment and machines. Also work with environmental specialists and evaluate several testing programs.

*Psychiatric Nurse*—The frontline for helping people with mental handicap needs and dealing with their environment. They usually have to help train those with a variety of needs from the most simple to a possible return to a return to the community/work force. Often tasked to help or take part in Group Therapies and certain types of Psychotherapy.

*Probation or Parole Officers*—Helping those with criminal pasts to readjust to life and avoid contacts and habits that have put them into the correctional system. Can be both frustrating and rewarding work at times.

*Social Psychologist*—They mostly focus on social behavior, relationships, attitudes, and interactions. In a very research-oriented world they are often the ones who are published in books, newspapers, magazines, and heard on radio and TV. Often hold academic positions and have allowances to perform in-the-field research.

Clinical Psychologist—The most popular career field in psychology. These doctors are the ones you would probably go to see for a problem of a mental nature. They practice various types of psychotherapy and group therapy.

# Chapter 2

## Psychological Method

One of the tenants of Psychology that makes it a true science is that the study mandates that research be conducted—and conducted in a true scientific manner. In conducting this research and performing experimentation some of the following are tools that need to be used...

*Natural Observation*—The process of observing and recording the behavior of organisms in their natural environment. This can be done with the use of tape recorders, video cameras, or simply recording the data manually.

*Directed Observation*—Done by observing behavior under controlled conditions in an experimental or laboratory setting.

*Case Study Method*—Involves detective-type work in order to provide objective descriptions of the background forces that may have influenced an individual's development.

*Interviews*—Collection of data through personal interviews. Some use a questionnaire format to keep data consistent, but often times the interviewer will go where the patient leads the conversation.

*Questionnaire Method*—A list of questions is developed on some subject and given to a selected group of individuals. Answers are usually collected in a statistical method for maximum input and analysis.

*Tests and Measurements*:

Aptitude Tests—Help to predict what individuals are likely to accomplish They receive training.

Achievement Tests—Measure how well you have mastered certain subject Matter.

*Experimental Method*: When this method is used by Psychologists they will usually start with a *Hypothesis* (tentative assumption or an "educated guess" that is often based on some previous research). The hypothesis always states a relationship between two or more *Variables* (condition or behavior that can change in amount or quality).

*Here are some terms and definitions that will help better understand the experimental process…

Independent Variable—Controlled and manipulated by the experimenter.
Dependent Variable—Changes in response to the independent variable.
Random Selection—Subjects have an equal chance of being assigned to either of the above groups.
Experimental Group—Group in which the condition under study is present.
Control Group—Group in which the condition is NOT present.
Theory—General principle, based on information, to explain what has been learned.
Subject—The organism (human or animal) participating in the experiment.
Anthropomorphism—When researchers attribute human characteristics to non-human beings.
American Psychiatric Association (APA)—The organization that has established controlling guidelines to protect subjects.
Hawthorne Effect—Subjects will act or respond differently if they know they are part of an experiment.

*Correlational Research*—Investigating the relationship between two variables.

Correlation—Refers to the consistent relationship between two sets of events or variables. Predictions can be made from these…

Positive Correlation—When changes in events or variables move in a similar direction.
Negative Correlation—When changes in events or variables move in opposite directions.

There is another, rather over-blown area linked to psychology but really does not include the scientific method that psychology does. But since it is a part of our world involving the mind and body lets take a look at what is sometimes referred to as a pseudo-science.

**Parapsychology**—"Para" means to the side of, or beyond and is concerned with psychological phenomena. It is normally divided into 2 parts:

*Cognitive*, which is more commonly referred to in its broadest area of phenomena known as Extrasensory Perception (ESP). Under this are several subdivisions of cognitive phenomena:

Telepathy—A person's awareness of another's thoughts without there being any communication through the sensory channel. (Sender-Receiver and Zenner Cards)

Clairvoyance—Knowledge acquired of an object or an event without the use of the senses. Involves one person and they are aware of an event or characteristics of an object.

Precognition—Knowledge a person may have of another person's future thoughts (precognitive telepathy), or of future events (precognitive clairvoyance).

*Physical*, which deals with phenomena like predicting the fall of the dice or willing cards to be dealt in a certain way. Still, the most popular in the physical area would be Psychokinesis (PK).

Psychokinesis—A person's ability to influence a physical object or an event. Things like bending a fork with your mind or moving a cup across a table…

Other types of phenomena that may, or may not be considered here are:

Spiritualistic phenomena (séance rooms & mediums)
Mental Healing (mentalists, faith healers, etc.)
Occultism and Vu Do
Prophesy
Psychics
Subliminal messages

# Unit II

## Developmental Influences

# Chapter 3

## Human Development

**Human Development**—It follows a predictable pattern as it spreads from head to feet and from the middle of the body outward. The responses that first develop are usually general, and then later will follow the specific responses. Development is a lifelong process as each stage develops its own unique features. It is also generally agreed that early development is more important than that which occurs in later years.

*Critical Periods*—The time periods during which an individual can learn specific behaviors most easily (ex. Language).

*Sensitive Periods*—When attachment and other stimulation from the environment is most important. (ex. 3 Reuses' monkeys)

**The Study of Development:**

*Longitudinal Method*—The process of selecting several individuals and studying the development of their behavior over a considerable period of time.
Drawbacks...

*Cross-sectional Method*—Where you select people of different ages in order to study groups of various levels.
Drawbacks...

**Types of Development:**

*Prenatal Development*—The development that takes place before birth. Some believe that this development begins at conception.

Physical Development—Growth of an individual's body such as height and weight (early vs. late, and male vs. female). Parents, siblings, friends, and teachers can also directly influence this growth.

*Motor Development*—The development of control over the muscles of the body. Self-image is a very important consideration as the person is very aware of how their development relates to others (awkward vs. coordinated). Abilities generally increase in the early to late twenties, and no ability is really lost as reach older adulthood—just speed and reaction time.

*Language Development*—In our world all languages have a vocabulary which consist of sounds and symbols.
- Animal communication
- Sign language
- Wild Boy of France and Genie

Language seems to develop in 4 stages:
1. Birth to 3 weeks—cries, coughing, and gurgles
2. 3 weeks to 5 months—cries vary in length, tone, and intensity
3. 5 months to 1 year—babbling sounds
4. 1 year and on—the language period

Facts about learning language:
- Rewards are important in learning
- Parents tend to correct words more than grammar
- Infants in other countries make similar early sounds
- Some disagreement on whether language is learned or biologically determined.

*Emotional Development*—This is how we develop an awareness and shows our expression of an affective (emotional) experience. This seems to show up in people that have unhappy emotions and how they can become unhappy people, and visa versa.

When certain emotions become present:
- Infancy: Fear and "stranger anxiety". Reaction to danger.
- Young Children: Fear of strange people, unfamiliar animals & objects, and the dark.
- Older Children: Substitutive fears (social situations, lightning & thunder, and death)
- High School: Being "different" and failure.
- Adults: Loss of security (job, home, family, etc.)
- Older Adults: Losing their job (retirement?), financial problems, and death.

*Social Development*—How we learn to act and live in a society as a member of that society. This involves habits, customs, right & wrong, the influence of others, and getting along with others.

When socialization becomes present:
- Birth: Starts immediately
- Preschool: Dependence (early), resistance (2 years), and cooperation
- Early School: Conformity, or adopting the standards of their age group
- Adolescents: Independence, interest in the opposite sex
    1. Hero-worship (Older, TV/Movie/Music/Sport stars, etc.
    2. Puppy-love (7th grade to Middle school ages)
    3. Romantic love (more intense and mature affections)
- Adulthood: Additional education associations, job acquaintances (marriage and raising a family)
- Older Adults: Adjusting to loss of job and retirement

*Intellectual (or Cognitive) Development*—The development of an individual's mental abilities.
Jean Piaget (1896-1980)—Swiss Psychologist that studied development of intelligence, reasoning, and thinking.

*Jean Piaget*

**Piaget's 4 stages of intellectual development:**

1. <u>Sensory-motor Period</u>: Develop senses and various muscular movements to interact with the environment (birth to 2 years).
2. <u>Preoperational Period</u>: Subject still lacks organization and is still self-centered (2 to 7 years).
3. <u>Concrete-operational Period</u>: Children start to think logically and realize that quantities remain the same although their shape may change (7 to 11 years).
4. <u>Formal-operational Period</u>: No longer self-centered, they are still concerned with their own problems. They now tend to use more possibilities to solve even the most abstract problems (11 years and older).

Moral Development—The development of the knowledge of what is right and wrong.

Lawrence Kohlberg (1927–)—One of the first Developmental Psychologists that put moral development into 6 stages.

Stage 1: Avoiding punishment.

Stage 2: Realizing what behaviors will benefit them, bring them rewards, or cause someone to return a favor.

Stage 3: What behaviors will please or help others and avoid their disapproval.

Stage 4: Develops a respect for authority and one's duty as a citizen.

Stage 5: More of a focus on the welfare of the community and the rights of others.

Stage 6: Start to base judgements on their own sense of right and wrong and principles of justice.

# Chapter 4

## Nature vs. Nurture

This chapter deals with the age-old question of is it "nature or nurture"? My belief is that it is BOTH heredity and environment that determines the person we will become and the behaviors we exhibit.

*Heredity*—These are the characteristics that are transmitted from parents to children before birth.

*Environment*—The surrounding forces that affect our lives.

**Contributing factors to our physical development:**

*Chromosomes*—Tiny rod-shaped bodies. Each human cell normally contains 46 chromosomes. We get 23 from the father's sperm, and 23 from the mother's egg—which gives us 23 pairs, or the 46 we've already mentioned.

*Genes*—Each chromosome is composed of many smaller units, called genes. They are responsible for the transmission of inherited traits from parents to children.

*Dominant Gene*—This is the gene that will determine if an individual will show a particular characteristic or trait that is controlled by that gene.

*Recessive Gene*—This gene will determine a characteristic or trait only if the gene on the matching chromosome is also recessive (ex. Eye color).

(*Note: A misconception might also be that you inherit traits like size, hair color, or other specific traits strictly from our parents—when in reality we are a composition of traits from a long genetic line from family lines.)

**Miscellaneous factors that affect development:**

*Selective Breeding*—The process of how we have manipulated genetics to produce changes in size, behavior, etc. Long used in the development of plants and animals (humans?).
- Embryonic Cells
- Cloning

*Identical Twins*—, As we know, they come from a single fertilized egg and have the same genetic makeup (gender, hair & eye color, etc.). Identical twins have long been studied in psychology for a number of factors from personality to intellect.

*Fraternal Twins*—Coming from two separate eggs, these are children who merely happen to be born at the same approximate time.

*Genetic Counseling*—A profession that can offer advise on having children when there is a suspected problem, defect, or something that is discovered in their genetic makeup.

*Maturation*—In our development, this is a pattern of individual growth that appears pretty much automatically as we grow older. Some of these developmental changes we see are in simple everyday activities like walking, language, learning, and how we interact with the environment.

>   *Environmental influences that also affect or influence our development are:
>   -   Chemicals in the mother's body
>   -   Use of tobacco products (pre and post birth)
>   -   Use of alcohol
>   -   Diet and body weight of the mother (prenatal)
>   -   Family and social relationships

Studies that have been done in a Restricted, Neutral, and Enriched environment have also taught us a great deal about how environment can also influence us.

# Chapter 5

## Biological Influences

In this chapter we will look at examples of how different aspects of our existence affect our body and our behavior.

Central Nervous System (CNS)—Made up of the Brain and Spinal Cord.

Peripheral Nervous System (PNS)—A large and complex system of nerve fibers that spread out through our body from the CNS.

Autonomic Nervous System (ANS)—Actually a sub-section of the CNS and PNS, it regulates the activities of the vital organs. Subsections of the ANS are the Sympathetic and Parasympathetic nervous systems.

Neuron—Nerve Cell.
- Sensory neuron: Receives and carries sensory information
- Motor neuron: From the brain, it carries messages to muscles

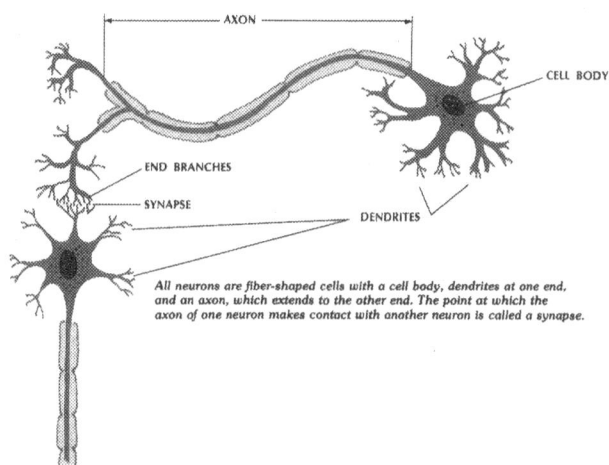

All neurons are fiber-shaped cells with a cell body, dendrites at one end, and an axon, which extends to the other end. The point at which the axon of one neuron makes contact with another neuron is called a synapse.

4 Basic Parts of the Neuron:
1.    Dendrites: Receive the nerve impulses
2.    Cell Body: Contains the neuron's chromosomes and genes
3.    Axon: Transmits messages to other neurons
4.    Synapse: Point at which two neurons meet (gap)

**Brain:**

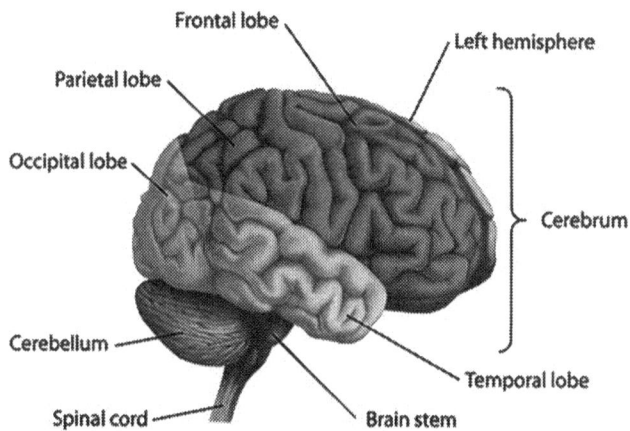

Here are 5 ways or techniques that are used to study how brain-to-behavior relationships might have been compromised:

1.  Stimulation: Neuro-stimulators at a specific part of the brain
2.  Brain Lesions: Damage to the brain caused by accident, surgery, or disease.
3.  Recording: Recording brain activity using EEG, PET, etc.
4.  Nerve tracing: Look for decayed or damaged nerves that are connected to the brain.
5.  Biochemical studies: Doing a chemical analysis of various levels in the brain that affect normal and abnormal behavior.

*Cerebral Cortex*—This is the highest brain center in humans. It is the thick layer of gray-colored (gray matter) neurons just under the skull. The highly important part of the brain contains information that makes you, you! It also helps to process sensory information and motor activities.

*Left/Right-side Brain Analysis*:
-   Right side: Controls spatial relationships, perceptions, fantasy, and creativity.
-   Left side: Controls language and logical thought.

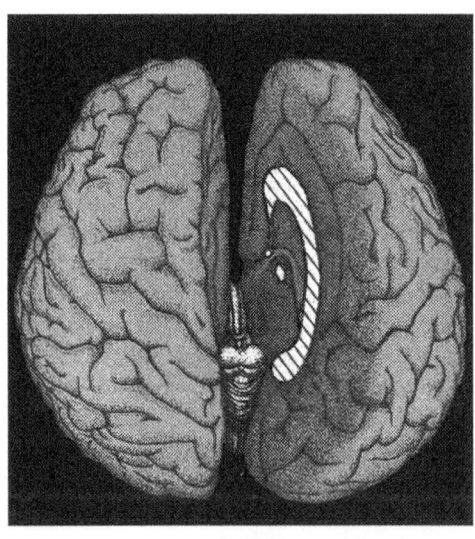

*Corpus Callosum*—Brain fibers that connect the two hemispheres of the brain.

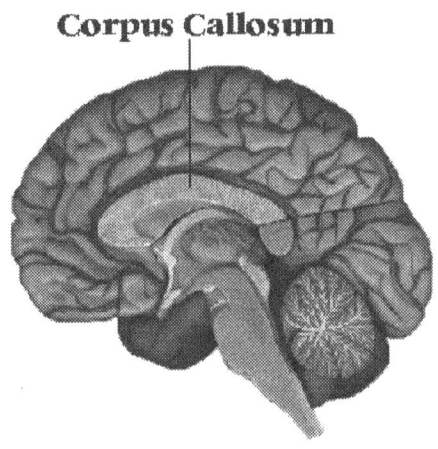

*Instruments* used to evaluate brain activity and abnormalities:
- Electroencephalogram (EEG)

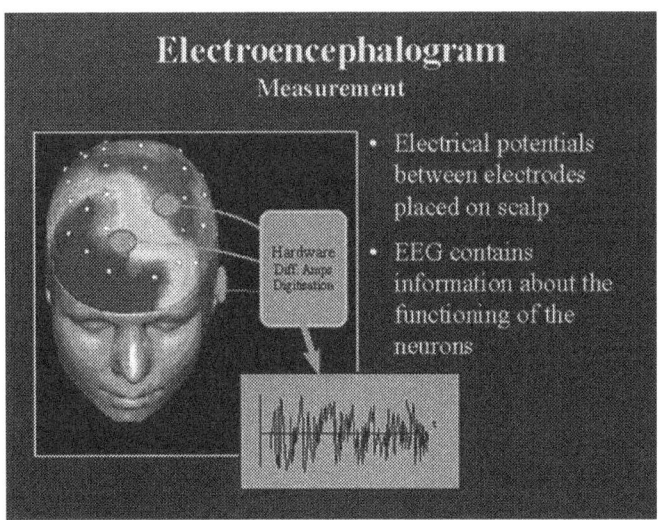

- CT Scan
- Positron Emission Tomography (PET)

*Glands*: These biological contributors to our psychological makeup determine our growth, energy levels, moods, and reactions to outside stimulus.

- <u>Duct Glands</u> (or Exocrine glands)—Empty their contents through small openings, or ducts (ex. Sweat and tear glands).
- <u>Ductless Glands</u> (or Endocrine glands)—These have no openings or ducts which they can pour their contents (ex. Thyroid and Pituitary glands).

Since the Endocrine glands have the greatest impact on our psychological behavior, lets look at them more closely...

## Endocrine System

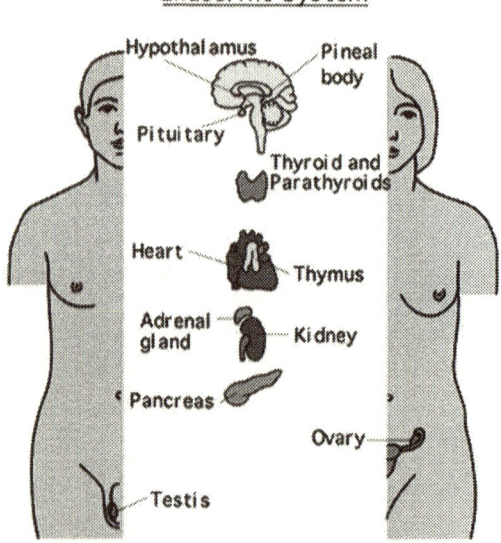

*Thyroid Gland*—Located in front of the windpipe, it produces hormones that regulate the speed of chemical reactions and the rate of growth.

- Hyperthyroidism: Too much thyroxin
- Hyperthyroidism: Too little (cretinism)

*Pituitary Gland*—Also known as the Master Gland, it is located on the underside of the brain and controls outputs from the other endocrine glands. The pituitary hormone (HGH) also controls the amount of growth (Too much = Giantism, Too little = Small people).

*Adrenal Gland*—Located just above each kidney and produces different hormones like adrenaline and cortisone that affects both mind and body.

*Gonads*—These supply the sperm (males) and the eggs (female) that are necessary for reproduction. These gonadatropic hormones also produce hormones that affect the development of our personalities. They are on a particularly high increase during adolescence.

**Sleep and Dreams:**

In the study of sleep we need to consider the effect, amount, change in patterns, and dreams to understand the profound effect this has on our behavior.

- Loss of sleep: Can vary with age in amount we need and how we might lose sleep at times.
- Short Naps: Studies done that show the positive effects of short naps during the course of a day.
- Change in the sleep cycle: Because of work or weekend plans, etc.

*5 Stages of Sleep:*
- Stages 1 through 4: Known at non-rapid eye movement or NREM sleep
- Stage 5: Known as rapid eye movement or REM sleep. Sometimes called paradoxical sleep this is when we experience dreams.

*Dreams*—As stated already, these will usually occur during stage 5 and can last for just a few minutes or for as much as an hour although the average dream lasts about 25 minutes. Everyone dreams and everyone needs to dream for proper mental health.

We will discuss dreams in much more detail after this chapter, but here are some facts about the subject of dreams at various ages:

- 3 to 4 year olds: Animals and Home
- 5 to 6 year olds: Broad range of activities and feelings (Girls tend to have mostly pleasant dream subjects, and Boys are more likely to experience unpleasant dreams like nightmares)
- 7 to 8 year olds: More pleasant subjects reappear
- 9 to 10 year olds: School settings and happiness
- 11 to 12 year olds: About people of their own age
- 13 to 14 year olds: Other people and their emotions (ex. Anger)

*Sleep Disorders:*
- Apnea: Halting of breathing, gasping.
- Idiopathic Hypersomnia: Constant state of drowsiness.
- Cataplexy: Temporary paralysis while awake.
- Myoclonus: Kicking of legs, arms while sleeping.
- Insomnia: Inability to fall or stay asleep.
- Narcolepsy: Instantaneously falling asleep.

*Parasomnias:*
- Sleepwalking
- Sleeptalking
- Night Terrors

*Hypnosis*—This is an unusual state of consciousness that has some similar features to sleep, but is not sleep. In this state you are open to "suggestion", and can carry out simple tasks and directions.

Methods of inducing the state of hypnosis:
- Flashing light or strobe
- Sounds or objects (metronome or shinny object)
- Spoken word (Hypnotist)

Some practical uses for hypnosis:

1. Treating patients with painful illnesses, injuries, or burns.
2. Can be used instead of a chemical anesthetic for minor surgeries
3. Treating certain types of mental illness and disturbances (ex. Phobias)
4. Helping eliminate undesirable behaviors (ex. Smoking and Drinking)
5. Finding lost items
6. Helping to bring out repressed memories

# Appendix A

## Dream Analysis

**History of Dream Studies:**
- Sigmund Freud
- Eugene Aserinsky
- Jung, Stekel, London, and Crisp

**Dream Log:** (*Assignment)
The dream log is a nightly record of dreams and the 4 main subject areas that are *characters, objects, settings, and actions*. By keeping a pad of paper near your bed to record the dreams during the night, or to write them down immediately in the morning—try to write down key ideas that will stimulate the memory of those dreams for additional information.

Here are some additional techniques to help with your dream log assignment…

1. Try to focus on the 4 main subject areas that will help with your analysis:
    A. <u>Characters:</u> Friends, Co-workers, Family, Famous people, Strangers, Doctors, Professional people, and Yourself (try to note in what "person" you are dreaming in). Try to note their names as well. List non-humans also.
    B. <u>Objects:</u> As many inanimate objects as you can recall.
    C. <u>Setting:</u> Where did these dreams take place?
    D. <u>Actions:</u> What was taking place? Emotions?
2. Write them down as soon as you wake—everything you can remember. Dreams fade very quickly.

3. Review everything as soon as you can and add some text to the key things you have already written down.
4. Don't try to analyze it write away—give yourself a few hours to evaluate it more objectively.
5. Go through and underline all the characters, objects, settings, and actions—then look up the possible symbolisms in your dictionary.
6. Look for reoccurring words and themes. Some dreams will interrelate and have even more meaning.
7. Important—be honest and don't embellish.

Important things to look for:
1. Recurrent Characters or Themes
2. Recurrent Patterns of symbolism
3. Familiar persons in unusual roles
4. People you normally would not think of
5. Yourself in an unusual role
6. Your or others in another age or life situation
7. Events with no relevance or are very vague
8. Be aware of possible "current event" dreams
9. Violence & Fear Reactions—Nightmares are VERY significant
   *"Other" factors that can be a part of your dreams…*
   - You will sometimes dream in fragments
   - Some dreams will move more quickly than they should, this is called "pictorial shorthand".
   - Some dreams will be forgotten. They might be unimportant, the message just wasn't that strong, or you just have problems with recalling after you awaken.
   - Some dreams can be affected by medications, when you are sick, or by what you've had to eat or drink.
   - You can sometimes "control" what you will dream about that night…

Here are some other types of dreams that haven't met the burden of proof as being a scientific fact:
   - Lucky dreams
   - Psychic dreams
   - Dream visualizations or training dreams

# DREAM DICTIONARY

## A

Abandoned—feelings of others at childhood (esp. parents); finding a new freedom.

Accident—anxiety; hidden aggression.

Address—present style of life, or who you were.

Airplane—(crashed) anxiety, (journey) shows a move, (grounded) not getting anywhere.

Alcohol—changes the way we feel, negative or positive feelings.

Alone—sense of isolation.

Angel—relationship with your mother; feelings about death; need for a parent figure to guide.

Animals—represents all our biological needs and responses.
    Ape—lost experiences
    Ass—plodding along, suffering
    Bear—power
    Bull—drives toward parenthood
    Cat—female sexuality
    Cow—female side of one's nature
    Dog—sexuality, friendship, devotion
    Elephant—power of life, growth & activity
    Frog—transformation
    Horse—pleasurable energy, dynamic sexual drive
    Lamb—childlike
    Lion—physical strength, temper
    Monkey—foolishness, thoughtlessness
    Mouse—minor irritations, fears & worries
    Pig—physical appetites
    Rabbit—sexuality, breeding, softness, & non-aggression
    Rat—sick or negative inside self

Wolf—fear
Artist—creative side

Ascending—rising feelings

Audience—standing in front of (attention, important); in audience (witness)

Autumn—something ending

## B

Baby—possessiveness, innocent, helplessness, lack of responsibility

Balloon—party mood

Banana—male penis

Band—teamwork

Bank—resources, security

Bath—relaxation, cleansing

Beach—family gatherings or relaxation; boundary or threshold

Bell—warning

Bicycle—effort or motivation which gets you somewhere

Birds—imagination, intuition, awareness
    Black bird—death
    Chicken—nourishment
    Dove—peace
    Eagle/hawk—dominance
    Owl—our intuitive sense
    Peacock—pride

Bite—aggression

Blindness—unwillingness to 'see' something

Boat, ship—journey through the seas of life

Body—whose? Identity.
    Abdomen—natural drives, hunger
    Anus—self expression and pleasure
    Arms—love, giving, taking, reaching
    Back—strength
    Blood—energy, existence
    Chest—place to store emotions
    Hair—thoughts, self image
    Hand—self expression, opportunity
    Head—thoughts, intellect
    Legs—support, motivation
    Muscles—strength
    Neck—weak point
    Pelvis—sexuality and sensuality
    Penis—drive of life
    Shoulders—to bear or to carry weight
    Skin—contact with the world
    Vagina—urges, ability to procreate

Bomb—explosive situation

Book—memories, things learned

Bread—nourishment, biological needs

Bride—feelings about or desire for marriage

Bridge—crossing from one phase of life

Bullet—sexual impregnation, aggression

Burial—letting go of the past

## C

Cage, cell—lack of opportunity, restrain

Calendar—taking notice, memory

Cancer—fear of this illness, eating away at

Car—our motivating drives, whatever is driving us in life

Cards—opportunity, fate

Cave—prenatal life, vagina, being lost

Cemetery—thoughts & feelings on death

Chain—restriction, strength, dependence

Chased—pursued by fears or emotion

Choke—conflict, indecision

Church—religious feelings or beliefs

Cigar, cigarette—masculinity, penis

City—society, community

Cliff—on the edge, facing fear

Clock—timing, urgency

Clothes—our feelings, anxiety, moods
    Apron—mother role
    Belt—restrained
    Blouse/shirt—feelings and emotions
    Coat—public 'self'
    Dress—femininity
    Gloves—protection
    Hat—opinions, mental attitudes
    Shoes—position in life, chosen direction
    Trousers—maleness
    Underclothes—intimate sexual feelings

Clouds—(bright) uplift, (dull) depression

Coffee—stimulating

Coffin—one's own mortality

Cold—emotions, fear

Colors—emotions and feeling tones
    Black—unknown
    Blue—depression
    Brown—depression, earthiness
    Green—growth, positive change
    Red—anger, passion
    White—awareness, purity, cleanness
    Yellow—cowardice

Comb—tidy up your thoughts

Cooking—nourishing oneself, creativity, giving

Cord—a restriction

Corridor—limbo, going from one thing to another

Countryside—a relaxed state

Crossing—a change

Crowd—public opinion

Crown—success

Cup—offering oneself

# D

Dam—'bottle up' emotions

Dancing—happiness, sexual mating

Danger—most often anxiety

Dark—unknown, secrets, death

Day—mostly our mood, 'seeing'. Night—secrecy, emotional hurt, lonliness

Death—something might die, lost opportunities

Defecate—self expression, release of tension, getting rid of

Departing—breaking away from

Descending—loss of status, aging, failure or death

Desert—loneliness

Digging—discovering and uncovering

Dirty—grubby or immoral

Diving—taking a chance

Divorce—anger towards one's spouse, break-up

Doll—target for violence, feeling about ourselves, wanting to be loved

Drink—to absorb or take something

Drowning—fear of being overwhelmed

Drunk—loss of control, lack of reason

## E

Earthquake—insecurity, breakdown of opinion

Eating—satisfying one's needs

Egg—potential

Empty—generally lack of

Enclosed—traps or restraints

End—a goal, release, death

Enter—new experience or new area

Evening—relaxation, quiet peace

Exams—self criticism, worry about some coming test

Explosion—anger, release of energy, orgasm

*F*

Failure—comparison, competitiveness

Fairground—public activity

Falling—*most common theme in dreams. Insecurity, big danger, death, loss of confidence, loss of control.

Family—patterns of relationships
    Father—authority
    Mother—uniting spirit of family
    Siblings—qualities in ourself, family
    Daughter—relationship with the daughter
    Son—extroverted self, feelings for the son
    Wife—sexuality, relationship with…
    Husband—sexual and emotional desire, relationship with…
    Grandparents—family traditions
    Relatives—the person dreamt about

Famous people—one's own potential

Farm—our natural drives, down-to-earth side of self

Fat person—feelings of inadequacy, jolly feelings

Fence—social barriers, privacy, territorial feelings

Fight—anger or frustration, desire to hurt, independence

Find—discover, realize, become aware of…

Fire—passion, sexuality, anger

Fish—unconscious physical and psychological impulses
    Jellyfish—helplessness, spinelessness
    Octopus—feeling trapped by mother
    Shellfish—avoiding hurt in sexual or emotional involvement
    Whale—powerful drives

Floating—relaxation, being carried along

Flowers—sense of beauty, feelings of pleasure, youthfulness

Flying—gaining of independence, escape, feelings of pleasure, transcendence

Fog—confusion, indecision

Follow—influenced, attraction to, seek something

Food—nourishment
    Bread—everyday life
    Cake—enjoyment
    Fruits—experience or effort
    Meat—physical or worldly satisfaction or needs
    Milk—self giving
    Olive—peace, kindness
    Sweets—sensual pleasure, special love

Fountain—process of life, flow of consciousness

Funeral—one's own death, warning

Furniture—attitudes or habits
    Bed—marriage, sex, rest
    Carpet—financial state
    Chair—passive, relaxed attitude
    Cupboard/closet—memories, resources
    Table—social connection with others

## G

Gambling—taking risks with your life, health, family

Garden—growth or change

Ghost—memories, feelings, guilt, which haunt us

Girl—feelings

Giving—relatedness, exchange

Glass—invisible yet tangible barriers

Glasses—ability to see, understand

Grave—concepts of death

## H

Heaven—life after death, retreat from life, harmony

Hell—self created misery

Hero—initiative and unexpressed potential

Hiding—being protective, feeling threatened

Hill—(uphill) difficulties, hard work; (downhill) might lose control

Holding—control, ownership, in touch with, responsibility, intimacy

Hole—a situation you might fall into, feel protected in

Homosexuality—desire for the father or mother's love, anxiety about one's gender

Honey—pleasure, sweetness

Horns—protectiveness, desire to hurt, sexuality (penis)

Hose—intestines, penis

House—depicts one's body
    Attic—the mind, memories
    Basement—sexual drive, kill ambition
House (cont.):
    Castle—defensive
    Chimney—smoking, inner warmth
    Church—moral rules, inner feelings
    Door—a boundary, escape (open or closed?)
    Hall—how you relate to groups
    Home—shelter, warmth, nourishment. Family
    Hospital—needing/involved in healing process
    Hotel—temporary attitudes, short term situation
    Hut—childhood family feelings
    Mansion—possibilities
    Roof—protecting ourself
    Room—a particular feeling state
    Stairs—towards something, going up or down?
    Wall—codes you live within, boundries
    Warehouse—memories
    Window—being aware of things

Hunger—our needs

## I

Ice—being cold or emotionally or sexually

Igloo—a cold, unloving home environment

Illness—painful memories, anger or resentment

Imprisoned—may be trapped, fear of failure

Insects—irritations or feeling something bugging you
    Wasp/hornets—painful emotions
    Lice/parasites—selfish
    Spider—emotions & conflicts one feels 'caught in'

Invisible—being forgotten

Iron—strength

Island—feelings of isolation or lonliness

# J

Jewelry—love given or received, something valuable

Jewels—treasures
    Amethyst—healing
    Diamond—human greed, hardness
    Emerald—personal growth
    Opal—fantasies
    Pearl—inner beauty
    Ruby—emotions, passion
    Sapphire—religious feelings

Journey—life and its ups and downs

Judge—decision making

Jungle—feelings from the unconscious, confusion, non-social

# K

Key—an attitude, thought, or feeling opening up areas

Kick—self assertion

Kill—repressing or stopping

King—one's father

Kiss—acceptance of…

Knot—tangle of feelings or tension

**L**

Ladder—your feelings, reaching towards something

Laugh—release of tension, ridiculing or feeling embarrassed

Letter—unrealized feelings, hopes, contact

Light—being aware, waking

Lighthouse—warning of danger

Lightning—unexpected changes, discharge of tension

Losing something—a lost opportunity

Lost—depicts confusion

Love—usually a direct expression of that feeling
    Baby love—completely dependent
    Adolescent love—uncertainty or clumsiness
    Adult love—recognizing needs of partner

Luggage—habits or attitudes

**M**

Mad—feeling threatened

Maggots—impurities in body; sickness

Make-up—change the impression we make on others, cover-up

Man—aspect of self (even in women…)
    Older man—father
    Man in woman's dream—her strength
    Man she knows or loves—feelings
    Two men—triangle

Map—clarification of a direction in life

Marriage/wedding—consider or experiment with idea; fear of…

Marsh/swamp—bogged down, held back

Mary, Virgin—motherhood

Mask—our false self

Maze—confusion, difficulty finding our way

Medicine—healing influence

Mermaid—idealized sense of womanhood

Metal—hardness of feelings

Microscope—introspection

Milk—human kindness, mother love

Mines—the unconscious

Mirror—concern over one's image; self love

Money—what we value; potential; (not enough, stolen?)

Monster—emotions or drives we are frightened of

Moon—love; romance

Motorbike—youthful drive; daring

Mountain—something big

Mud—basis of life; hopelessness or despair

Muscle—feelings and forces in our being

Musical instrument—one's sexual organs or skills in self-expression

## N

Nail—bonding; holding power

Navel—dependency

Necklace—special qualities

Needle—penetrating insight

Nest—emotional dependence upon parents; home life

Newspaper—news to you; need to be aware of…

Nude—dropping the façade

Numbers—personal meanings
    1—one's self
    2—duality
    3—triangle
    4—physicality, stability & strength

    5—the human body
    6—harmony or sex
    7—cycles of life
    8—death & resurrection; infinity
    9—pregnancy, childbirth
    10—new beginning
    11—eleventh hour

    12—a year
    13—bad luck

    0—the female; absolute or hidden

# O

Oar—personal energy

Oats—sexual energy

Obstacle—causes uncertainty or withdrawal of enthusiasm

Office—relationship at work

Officer/official—authority or officialdom; father; right & wrong

Oil—removes friction

Operation—actual operation; a sick inner attitude

Orphan—abandoned or unloved

Ostrich—avoidance of seeing

Oven—pregnancy or the womb; one can change

# P

Painting—subtle feelings or realizations; expression of feelings

Pan/pot—creativity, family life

Paper—unexpressed sentiments (blank), how others see you (wrapping)

Paralysis—fears we have; guilt or inadequacy

Party—feelings about groups; social skills or lack of it…

Passenger—carried along; moved by someone else; responsibility

Path—decided on or is following

Pen/pencil—desire to communicate

Pepper—livening up; irritation

Perfume—(good) good feelings, (bad) bad emotions

Perspire/sweat—mostly fear

Pet—our natural drives and feelings or caged (depends on dream)

Photos—memories

Pill—experience you need; something good for you

Pillow—comfort; feeling alone (hugging)

Pimple—character blemishes

Pipe—connections with others

Pit—situations one finds difficult to get out of

Planets—abstract
    Sun—energy
    Moon—*see moon
    Mercury—intuition
    Venus—love
    Mars—energetic activity

Plants—progressive change

Plate—needs, appetites

Playing—might just be fun or suggest great seriousness (depends on the game)

Plowing—changing oneself; new growth

Plunge—taking a risk

Pocket—personal secrets or thoughts

Poison—warning to avoid something

Positions—stance or life
>    Above—superior
>    Behind—the past
>    Below—'beneath you'
>    Close—intimacy
>    Distant—does not identify with strongly
>    In front—the future
>    Opposite—resistance
>    Side—supportive feelings

Postures (movement)
>    Jump—daring
>    Kneel—humility
>    Prone—relaxation
>    Run—exuberance
>    Sit—relaxed; inactive waiting
>    Squatting down—sleep, rest
>    Standing—what one 'stands for'
>    Turn—a change
>    Walk—motivation and confidence

Poverty—being inadequate

Pregnancy—one's potential or personality developing; desire for a child

Presents—(receiving) being affirmed, (giving) giving of self

Prince—best of dreamer (male)

Princess—best of dreamer (female)

Prize—feeling rewarded

Prostitute—dire sexual need; deadening moral restrictions

Pulling—positive action, expression of will

Puppet—manipulation

Purse—something we value and try not to lose

Pushed/pushing—taken for granted; getting what you want

## Q

Quarrel—conflict within

Quicksand—insecurity

## R

Race—competitiveness

Rain—depressed feelings or difficulties

Rainbow—better things to come; beauty; value of life
Reading—realization; recall from memory

Record (cassette, CD, disk)—pleasure, impressions.

Refrigerate—cool down our emotions

Reptiles/lizards/snakes—attraction or repulsion…
    Frog—growth process
    Lizard—same as snake with no 'poisonous' aspect
    Snake—worries about our health; life process; (in a hole) sexual
    Toad—feel squeamish about or ugly side of ourselves

Rescue—intervention

Restaurant/café—sociability

Ring—one's 'wholeness'

River—flow and events of our life or destiny

Road—prevailing direction in or approach to life

Rock—reality, stability

Roles—characters in our dreams…
    Actor/actress—wanting acclaim, expression
    Authority figure—use of power, leadership
    Captive/prisoner—denying free expression
    Carpenter—creative, but practical part of us
    Cook—the active and practical side of our nature
    Dentist—fear of being hurt
    Doctor—dependence upon authority figure
    Farmer—practical down-to-earth feelings
    Fireman—passions or outbursts of emotion
    Nun—sexual purity
    Pirate—plundering urges
    Policeman/woman—socially right or wrong
    Sailor—meet the storms and calms of life
    Salesman—opportunity
    Scientist—creative rational mind
    Secretary—other woman; business side
    Soldier—in conflict with
    Stranger—unknown aspect of something
    Teacher—learning situation
    Thief—something gained or taken

Rope—holding us back

Rust—negligence; aging

S

Sand—lack of security

Satellite—more global awareness

Savings—sense of security

School—the learning process

Scissors—cutting remarks; anger; separation

Sea—human experience of known and unknown

Searching—attempt to find

Sewing—creating; changing

Shampoo—clear away

Shop—desires; something you want

Signature—agreement

Silence—uneasiness

Sing—expressing one's inner feelings

Sinking—despairing; losing ground

Sky—the mind

Sleeping—surrender of waking self

Smoke—danger

Smoking—anxiety

Snow—coldness; pureness; beauty

Soap—'clean up'; clearing away

Space—opportunity, independence & freedom

Speed—intensity of feelings

Spring—new growth

Statue—unresponsive or cold

Stone—hardness, unfeeling

Storm—anger

Sugar—pleasure

Suicide—lack of pleasure in life

Summer—mid-life; pleasure; warmth

Swimming—confidence in dealing with the emotions

Syringe—intercourse; other people's opinions; drug dependence

*T*

Talking—expressing what one feels and thinks

Tangled—confusion

Tattoo—indelible memory

Tea—sociability

Teddy bear—desire for comfort

Telephone—attempt to communicate

Telescope—a 'closer' look

Television—what is going on

Tent—natural forces, getting away

Tests—measuring oneself; self assessment

Thunder—repressed emotions; outbursts

Ticket—get somewhere; confidence

Tickle—release tension

Time of Day—passage of time
    Daylight—waking conscious life
    Afternoon/evening—end of life; middle or old age
    Hours of the day—age
    Midday—midlife
    Morning—our youth
    Night—memories or mysteries; painful areas; search

Toilet—privacy

Tomato—passion; sexuality

Tomb—feelings or insights about death

Tools—practical abilities
    Drill—working through the emotions
    Hammer—aggression
    Saw—energy to reshape

Tornado—we feel powerless

Tortoise—shyness; withdrawal

Toy—childhood attitude; just 'playing'

Transparent—something we can 'see through'

Traveling—what you are doing with your life

Treasure—riches of the self

Trees—living structure of our inner self
    Oak—strength
    Flowering—fertility
    Fruit—production
    Christmas—eternal aspect

Trespassing—not respecting someone else's boundaries

Tunnel—innermost feelings; vagina

## U

Umbrella—ward off difficult feelings

Undress—reveal one's real feelings

Uniform—identification with a role; conformity

University—potential and learning ability; something important

Urine—release of sexual feelings; flow of life; need to pee!

## V

Valley—being down to earth; depression or gloominess

Vampire—fear associated with someone who is too demanding

Vanish—losing awareness

Vase—womb; receptivity

Vault—womb; store of resources

Village—quiet homely feelings

Vine—connections with family and ancestors

Violin—innermost feelings

Virgin—free of preconceptions; girlhood or innocence

Volcano—long held emotions or hurts

Vomit—discharge of feelings

Voyage—new undertaking

## W

Wall—our defensive attitudes; security; barriers

Wallpaper—surface appearance of things

War—internal conflicts
Washing—getting rid of negative feelings

Watch—time; present

Water—emotions, moods and flow of feelings

Weapons—desire to hurt someone
    Arrow—hurtful words or action; a message
    Gun—confidence; penis
    Knife—cutting, insight, penis
    Sword—erection, social power, justice

Weather—our moods and emotions

Web—a sticky situation

Weeds—not contributing much, stopping more positive growth

Weight—seriousness

Well—deepest resources of life

West—death; end of something

Wheat—wisdom of experience

Wheel—meet changes; to be mobile

Whip-hurtful remarks

Wig—false ideas

Wind—ideas and conceptions

Winter—emotional coldness; old age

Witch—fears or difficult feelings; problems with mother; vindictiveness

Wood—the past; habitual

Wool—warmth; gentleness

Work—one's work or lack of it; actively trying to change

Worm—feeling insignificant

Wound—hurt feeling; trauma from the past

Writing—thinking about something, expression, leaving your 'mark'

## X Y Z

X—an error; unknown quantity
Yawn—boredom; tiredness
Zoo—natural urges and instincts; social grouping; *see animals.

# Unit III

## Personality

# Chapter 6

## Personality

*Personality*—The sum total of an individual's "relatively consistent", organized, and unique thoughts and reactions to the environment.

- Relatively consistent: Most people have personality traits that do not change a great deal from day to day.
- Organized: So that we can get along with, and work with others
- Unique: We all seem to have different personalities that make us different from one another.

**Personality Development:**

*Early Childhood*—Most of these traits tend to be biologically determined. Some would say that what you learn early will stay with you the rest of your life, while others would say that your personality will undergo many changes through the years. Perhaps a little of both theories might be correct.

*Influences at Home*—Child Psychologists suggest that the more decisions a child is allowed to make, the quicker and more well rounded the personality seems to become. Yet, going back to an earlier discussion of the Sensitive Period—the amount of affection the child gets at home has a tremendous affect on personality development.

*Birth Order*—The social effect of where they are placed in the family could have an influence on how they are reared and how they might interact with others.

## *Birth Order*

**Quick Personality Quiz:**

*Which set of personality traits best fits you?*

    A.  Well organized, logical, serious, reliable, perfectionist, hard driving, critical.

    B.  Many friends, loyal to peers, mediator, independent, unspoiled, secretive.

    C.  Charming, attention-seeker, people person, engaging, manipulative, precocious.

    D.  Very thorough, self-motivated, high achiever, high expectations, fearful

**Some Statistics:**

- Middle children have the best record for lasting marriages
- Best Match? First born and Last born
- If two Last borns marry they are likely to go into debt
- Marriage between 2 Middle children can be the most destructive
- Middle and Last born are a good match also

**Information on Birth Orders:**

### *First Born Children:*
- Parents have more of a "critical eye" and can be hard on them
- Have the most conflicts with the Third born
- Usually end up being leaders, successful @ work, church, or other organizations. *Can work against you in personal relationships
- *Descriptive Words:*

| | |
|---|---|
| + Over protective | + Precise |
| + Anxious | + Picky |
| + Demanding | + People-pleasers |
| + Pushy | +Achieving |

+ Goal Oriented

## Middle Born Children: "Middle Child Syndrome"

- Can be a "closed book" to their family
- Mentally tough and independent
- Usually run with the pack
- Often feels left out
- Usually leaves home very quickly and becomes very spirited
- Tends to reject family do's and do not's—considered a rebel
- Descriptive Words:

| | |
|---|---|
| + Lower expectations | + Sociable |
| + Feels ignored | + Laid-back |
| + Feel insulted by family | + Easy-going |
| + Mysterious | + Avoids conflict |

+Goes their own way

## Last Born Children:

- Have a "we'll show them attitude"
- Typically outgoing, personable, manipulators
- Love affection and are uncomplicated
- Carefree people and usually popular
- Usually just out for admiration and getting laughs
- *Descriptive Words:*

| | |
|---|---|
| + Charming | + Rebellious |
| + Absent-minded | + Temperamental |
| + Clown or Entertainer | + Spoiled and Impatient |

## The Only Child:

- Tend not to see the humor in things
- Only trust their own opinion, and not afraid to make decisions
- They think they are always right
- *Descriptive Words:*

> + Confident                          + Ultra perfectionists
> + Articulate                         + Never satisfied
>              + Self-centered

*Society* (Large group of people who share common traits, customs, and ways of behaving)—Personality can be shaped by how we perceive society looks at us as individuals. Some of the factors that seem to play an important role in how we are evaluated would be Financial Success, Occupation, and Values.

**Personality Theory:** We seem to be evaluated on two levels…One is sometimes referred to as the "molecular" approach because it looks at personality in terms on smaller, more specific features of our behavior. The second would be the "molar" that would look at the larger, more general units of our behavior (much like the Gestalt theory).

*Factors that influence personality:*
-   Goals: Where does that person want to go with their lives or what is holding them back?
-   Effect of Reward & Punishment: Goes back to early childhood development where you do things to get rewards and avoid behavior that will get you in trouble.
-   Learning: How easily or how hard you have to work to achieve success (esp. in a school setting).
-   Heredity: The "nature" part of theory where you seem to carry on certain personality traits of our parents.
-   Early Childhood Experiences: More along the lines of the environmental theory where things that happen to you early on will stay with you throughout your life.
-   Unique Behavior: How different your behavior might be compared to the rest of society.
-   Environment: Family, Job, Church, School, and our Friends influence on things we do and the way we act.

Freud's (1856-1939) **Psychoanalytic Theory** of Personality:
  *Conscious level*—These are the thoughts we are aware of at any given moment.
  *Unconscious level*—The desires, wishes, needs, and impulses we may or may not be aware of.

*Freud's 3 Systems of Personality*:

1. Id—Theorized to be the original system, present when we are born. Also the source for the other 2 systems. This system works and acts according to the "pleasure" principle (low stress through receiving pleasure).

2. Ego—The conscious level that is the middle ground between the Id and the realities of the outside world. Works off of the "reality" principle.

3. Superego—This is another subconscious system that contains our values, right & wrong, and our ideals of society. Works on the "moral" principle.

*Because two of these systems involve the unconscious, Freud employed his 3 methods of psychoanalysis to help bring these out: Hypnosis, Free Association, and Dream Analysis.

Carl Jung's (1875-1961) **Analytical Psychology** Theory:

*Carl Gustav Jung*

*Jung's 2 levels of the unconscious:*
1. <u>Personal Unconscious</u>—Experiences that were once part of our conscious level but are now forgotten.
2. <u>Collective Unconscious</u>—Memories of our ancestors are still part of our unconscious memories.

*The 2 "Attitudes" of personality:*
1. <u>Introversion</u>—People who tend to respond more to internally oriented stimuli.
2. <u>Extroversion</u>—These people are more keyed into social situations and ideas from others, and respond more to external stimuli.

*People tend to mainly into one of these attitudes or another—here are the characteristics that might help you figure out which one you fall in to…

## Social Psychoanalytic Theorists:

*Alfred Adler* (1870-1937)—He referred to his study as "Individual Psychology", and although he was an associate of Freud's he believed we are mainly conscious beings and are greatly influenced by our social interactions. Probably the best known of his work was the identification of the "Inferiority" and "Superiority" Complexes.

Still, he considered the cornerstone of his theory to be based on what he called the "Creative Self", where we strive for complete fulfillment of our goals in life (similar to Humanistic theory).

*Alfred Adler*

Erich Fromm (1900-1980)—Stressed how much human society influences and affects the individual. Also, that there is interaction between our basic needs and the opportunities to fulfill them.

Fromm's *5 Specific Needs*:
1. Relatedness—In place of nature we replace it with people.
2. Transcendence—Creativity and rising above the norm.
3. Belonging—Our closeness to the world and other people.
4. Identity—Our desire to be unique.
5. Frame of Reference—How we view life.

*Erich Fromm*

*Karen Horney* (1885-1952)—One of the first to disagree with the theories of Freud. She would emphasize that there is a major social relationship that starts with the "Parent-Child" relationship. For example, if there were disturbances in the person's personality it was probably caused by the amount of love and security they felt as a child.

And much like Wundt, she also believed we have Inner Conflicts that need to be examined in order to resolve problems in our lives.

*Karen Horney*

*Harry Stack Sullivan* (1892-1949)—Included with the Social Psychoanalytic theorists because his belief that our personality exists from our contact and relationships with others.

Stack's 3 *Processes of Personality*:
1. Dynamism—The pattern of behavior that occurs over and over again, similar to a habit.
2. Personification—An image we have of Self or Others. These are sometimes reflected in our attitudes, feelings, and ideas.
3. Cognitive—These are the ways we think or interpret things based on symbols, sensations, and images.

*Erik Erikson* (1902-1994)—Gave us a timeline of how our personality develops.

Erikson's *8 Stages of Personality Development*:
1. Birth—1 year—Basic trust vs. mistrust.
2. 2–3 years—Achieving individuality & autonomy.

3.  4—5 years—Initiative vs. Guilt
4.  6—11 years—Industry vs. Inferiority
5.  Adolescence—Identity vs. Role confusion
6.  Young Adulthood—Intimacy vs. Isolation
7.  Middle Adulthood—Generativity vs. Stagnation
8.  Late Adulthood—Integrity vs. Despair

*Erik Erikson*

**Behavioristic Theorists:**

*B. F. Skinner* (1904-1992)—Studied personality in terms of behavior.
-   <u>Cause and Effect</u>: Cause—Environmental factors. Effect—Responses to those environmental factors.
-   <u>External Events</u>: Primarily those that can be measured.
-   <u>Reinforcement</u>: When rewards increase it will likely increase the occurrence of that behavior, and that when rewards decrease so will that type of behavior.
-   <u>Punishment</u>: Reward desirable behavior, but do not punish bad behavior—rather ignore it or do not reward it.

*Albert Bandura* (1925–)—Also based many of his theories on how we interact and learn from social behavior. Because of this the basis of a majority of his developmental theory was based on Observation-Imitation.

- <u>Models</u>: A person whom we use as an example. That we imitate behavior if a model is rewarded or has been rewarded in the past, and that the punishment of that model reduces the desire to imitate them.

**Humanistic Theorists:**

This school of theory emphasizes the positive aspects of human growth, and that we have an active drive toward Health, Growth, and Creativity. Also, that the environment (not nature) develops the so-called bad behavior.

*Abraham Maslow* (1908-1970)—Based his theories on the premise that we have various motivations to satisfy or meet certain needs.

Maslow's *Hierarchy of Needs*:
1. <u>Physiological Needs</u>: These involve things our bodies need to survive like food, water, air, rest, etc.
2. <u>Safety Needs</u>: The desire to avoid danger and to have security in our lives.
3. <u>Love and Belonging</u>: That we need and seek out affectionate relationships with other people.
4. <u>Self-Esteem</u>: Desire to be recognized and have a feeling of confidence.
5. <u>Knowledge and Understanding</u>: That we are a curious people needing to explore our environment and acquire more knowledge.
6. <u>Aesthetic</u>: Our desire for beauty, truth, perfection, and justice.
7. <u>Self-Actualization</u>: Striving to develop abilities that are currently undeveloped. To accept ourselves and others. To maintain a sense of humor. To be creative. To seek the welfare of others and to be less self-centered.

*Abraham Maslow*

*Table 1*
*Maslow's hierarchy of needs*

| Level | Type of Need | Examples |
|---|---|---|
| 1 | Physiological | Thirst, sex, hunger |
| 2 | Safety | Security, stability, protection |
| 3 | Love and Belongingness | To escape loneliness, love and be loved, and gain a sense of belonging |
| 4 | Esteem | Self-respect, the respect others |
| 5 | Self-actualization | To fulfill one's potentialities |

Carl Rogers (1902–1987)—As is generally the basis of most Humanists, he was also self-actualization oriented.

Self-Concept: This is a system of attitudes that people have toward themselves. In this concept we base a lot of our concept on emotions and feelings we have at the time. This idea also states that we are free to be ourselves, much like free will. Also, the extent to which we use the "I" principle will also reflect a great deal about ourselves and how egocentric or egoexpansive we might be.

Adjustment: How we resolve conflicts between our self-concept and reality. Do we look for excuses or explanations—do we attempt to change our concepts if it is in conflict with reality...

*Carl Rogers*

## Criticisms of these theories...

Psychoanalytic—Looks at behavior <u>after</u> it has already happened.

Social Psychoanalytic—"Society" is too difficult to change. Too idealistic.

Behavioristic—Says humans have no free will of their own.

Humanistic—How do you measure Self Concept, Emotion, and Feelings?

# Chapter 7

## Measuring Personality

There are many tools in place to measure personality and this chapter will give you a quick glimpse at some of the terminology and testing available to give insight into this area of psychology.

*Standardized Tests*—There are a number of these tests that are given, scored, and interpreted the same way by different evaluators.

*Norm Group*—The group of people similar to those who will take the test later.

*Reliability*—The degree to which the score or rank will be the same, or near the same. Although not perfect, the more reliable the test the better it is. Some of the factors that affect the reliability of the test are:
- Number of items on the test
- Emotional state of the subject
- How clearly the directions were given
- Physical surroundings
- Type of test

*Validity*—This determines if the test is measuring what it is supposed to measure. A test can be reliable, but not valid—and if it is not reliable it cannot be valid.

*Ratings*—After the test is given and scored you can now assign a rank or a score to that individual.

*Ranking Methods*—You can give the individual a "number" ranking, a percentile ranking, or other position to show a comparison that will give the individual some relevance to where they stand.

*Graphic Rating Scale*—To give a visual position of where the subject stands you could develop a bar chart, line chart, etc.

As an evaluator of a standardized test you have to be careful not to fall into some of the "human" interpretations that we sometimes fall in to…

- Overrating: Giving overly high ratings by the rater
- "Halo Effect": Rating high on all traits because of one favorable trait
- Stereotyping: A learned judgement based on a person's race, nationality, social group, sex, etc.
- Pigeonhole: When we categorize people in a certain way
- Attribution: Evaluating someone based on our own characteristics, or our opposite characteristics.

*Personality Inventory*—This will help you find out about various aspects of personality, or adjustments to their environment.
- Better done individually than in groups
- Tests can be biased or lied about (must be honest)
- Measures habits, and habits can change
- Should be used with other related information

*Interviewing*—This gives you the opportunity to have a one-on-one communication with the subject.
- Not always a valid way of measuring personality if the judgement of the interviewer is biased (more would be best)
- Tools that would be of assistance with this method would be having a list of questions already to go, a rating scale, and a recording device of some type (videocamera, etc.)

*Behavior Sampling*—A fairly new technique where you look at actual behavior to measure or record for evaluation purposes. These sample situations can be used to test their reaction when they might be placed in a real situation.

*Projection*—Although difficult to interpret, score, and administer (different psychologists interpret in different ways); people will sometimes attribute elements in their own personalities to other people or objects. Here are some of the projective techniques that have been used or are currently being used to help look into the deeper levels of why certain personality traits exist.

- Inkblot Tests: Herman Rorschach (Swiss Psychologist) developed the first test using 10 standard inkblots where any number of responses could be considered. The Holtzman Inkblots is a more recent test that utilizes 45 inkblots that should have only one standard response.
- Pictures and Stories: The subject will interpret a picture or complete a story that the evaluator starts.
- Figures on a Background Picture: The subject places figures or faces on the picture.
- Finger Painting: Evaluate the mannerisms and type of picture that is created.
- Toys: What type of toys and how they play with them.
- Complete the sentence: The subject will complete a statement that the evaluator starts for the purpose of opening areas in their lives.

*Achievement Tests*—Measures how much knowledge a person can report in a subject area—usually by use of a standardized test. Some of the subjects that are evaluated could be history, math, biology, language, reading, science, etc.

*Aptitude Tests*—These tests will judge if you are likely to succeed in a particular activity or skill.

*Vocational Interest Inventories*—This will give the subject feedback that will show similar interests to those who work in those jobs.

- Kuder Preference Inventory: This will have questions that are designed to show interest in these 10 vocational areas:

1.  Outdoor work
2.  Mechanical
3.  Computation
4.  Science
5.  Persuasion
6.  Art
7.  Literary work
8.  Music
9.  Social Service
10. Clerical

- <u>Strong-Campbell Interest Inventory</u>: More recent survey that takes into account many more vocational areas.

Some of the *disadvantages* of these inventories might be:

- People may not try a career if they receive low scores
- New interests might develop as you grow older
- Do not take into account "short term" interests
- Subjects might bias the results by intentionally answering in a certain way

*Person Centered Psychology*—We will cover this in greater detail when we cover Humanistic Psychology in more depth, but this means of evaluation looks more into goals and potential to succeed if given the proper opportunities. Based more on their own lives and the environment in which they live.

# Unit IV

## Intelligence, Learning, and Thinking

# Chapter 8

## Measuring Intelligence

*Intelligence*—The ability to adapt to new and old situations in the environment.

**Early Theorists on Intelligence:**

*L.L. Thurstone*—Developed the 7 main factors of intelligence.

1. <u>Space Factor</u>: How the subject interprets 3-dimensional forms and how they relate to basic forms.
2. <u>Number Factor</u>: Evaluates numerical tasks and mathematics
3. <u>Verbal Comprehension</u>: Understanding words and how they interpret verbal communication
4. <u>Verbal Fluency Factor</u>: How they express themselves orally or in written form
5. <u>Memory Factor</u>: How they recall learned information and facts
6. <u>Reasoning</u>: Ability to figure out a general rule
7. <u>Perceptual Factor</u>: Ability to grasp visual details, similarities, and differences

*J.P. Guilford*—Expanded the above to 120 factors
- Included creative and imaginative thinking
- Allowed for a "range" of intellectual abilities

Some of the *drawbacks* of these early theories:

- Can be high in one area, yet low in another affecting the over-all rating
- Doesn't explain how these different factors interact with one another
- There could be such a thing as a "general" intellectual ability

**Tests:**

Alfred Binet (1857-1911)—French Psychologists tasked by the French government to find out why some children did better in school than others.

- Initially worked with Theadore Simon in developing a 30-task test
- Eventually teamed up with Lewis Terman at Stanford University to develop the now famous and long-used Stanford-Binet Test of Intell.

**Individual Tests:**

*Wechsler Tests*—Still a popular test given in a number of different venues.

> WPPSI (Wechsler Preschool and Primary Scale of Intelligence) 4-6.5 years
> WISC-R (Wechsler Intelligence Scale for Children-Revised) 6.5-16 years
> WAIS-R (Wechsler Adult Intelligence Scale-Revised) 16 years and older

*Culture-Fair Tests*—There have been many complaints by minority populations that intelligence tests were designed for the middle-class, Caucasian population and is therefore unfair. This test measures different cultural backgrounds and differences that may exist in their past learning. It utilizes non-verbal, auditory memory, and picture completion.

**Group Tests:**

*CTMM* (California Test of Mental Maturity)—Measures language, non-language, and opposites/similarities.

*Otis-Lennon Mental Ability Test*—Puts emphasis on the verbal aspects of intelligence.

*\*Drawbacks*—Illness, emotions, poor directions, lack of motivation, and the opportunity to possibly cheat on these tests.

*Intelligence Quotient (I.Q.)*—The ratio between a person's chronological age and their mental age.

> Mental Age—Estimate of a person's level of mental functioning, usually based on an intelligence test.
> Chronological Age—Years, months, and days the subject has lived.

$$\text{I.Q.} = \frac{\text{Mental Age (MA)}}{\text{Chronological Age (CA)}} \times 100$$

*Because adult intelligence is difficult to measure because of the negative correlation of increasing years (CA), but without schooling or continued learning the mental abilities (MA) might actually decline. Therefore the *"Deviation I.Q."* was developed to compare age groups. Tests have indicated that when using this type of measurement the IQ tends to stay about the same.

*Types of Intelligence:*

> Fluid Intelligence—Mostly inherited abilities.
> Crystallized Intelligence—Acquired through interaction throughout our lives.
> *As we get older our F.I. decreases, while our C.I. increases.

*Uses of Intelligence Tests:*

> *Schools*—Used to predict student productivity and potential
> -    Elementary Schools: Tends to be a very close relationship between student achievement and their IQ.
> -    High School: Less closely related because lower IQ's tend to drop out, the subjects that are studied, jobs, extracurricular activities, and social lives.
> -    College Level: Even a smaller correlation due to similarities of distractions given above.

> *Occupational Environment*—Like in Elementary Schools, a close relationship seems to exist between job/salary levels and IQ.

**Mental Retardation** (About 2% of the population have an IQ below 70)

*The 4 Levels of MR:*
1.  Profound (IQ below 20)—Generally have Infant-like characteristics meaning they cannot wash, dress, eat, or take care of bodily needs by themselves.

2.  <u>Severe</u> (20-34)—Similar traits to that of a 3-year old.
3.  <u>Moderate</u> (35-49)—Can do the things an early elementary student can do (5-7).
4.  <u>Mild</u> (50-69)—Have a Mental Age of an 8 to 12 year old and can do a great deal of similar things that most of us can do to a certain extent.

*Causes of Mental Retardation* (There are over 150 suspected causes of MR, but these are the 4 main causation factors:

- Heredity
- Injury
- Dangerous chemicals before birth
- Genetic-Chromosomal

There is no "cure" for MR, but these can be helpful:

- Drugs
- Surgery
- Vitamins
- Psychotherapy
- Special Education
- Support and Understanding

**Superior Intelligence:**

*"Gifted"*—Usually evaluated as having an IQ of over 140 and defined as someone who in capable of producing good works that could influence all of mankind.

*"Prodigies"*—Those who have a mastery of one particular area.

"Savantism" (also Idiot Savant and "Rainman Syndrome)—Developmentally disabled with a special skill.

Other *Characteristics* of those possessing superior intelligence:

- Stand out academically

- Leaders in school
- Less self-centered
- Interested in the problems of society
- Well adjusted
- Lower suicide and divorce rates
- Make career plans earlier
- Healthier

# Chapter 9

## Learning

*Learning*—Lasting changes in behavior that occurs as a result of practice or past experience. Other types of learning occur based on Reflex (considered to be mostly an automatic type of behavior) and Physical Growth (which allows us to learn more based on muscle and nerve development).

**Classical Conditioning:**

- A type of learning that develops when certain stimulus brings forth a response that it did not previously evoke.
- Largely considered the development of *Ivan Pavlov* (1849-1936), a Russian scientist that studied this type of learning through early experimentation with dogs.

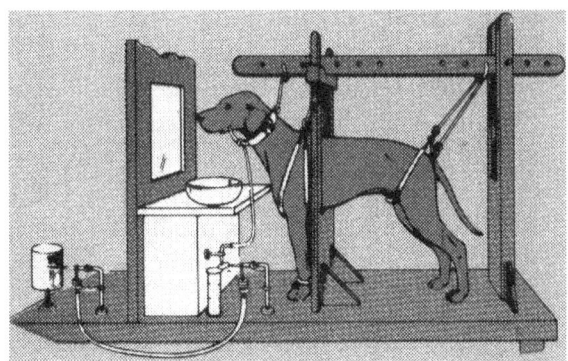

*Principles of Classical Conditioning:*
-   Unconditioned Stimulus (UCS)—Normal, unlearned agent.
-   Unconditioned Response (UCR)—Occurs normally with no learning necessary.
-   Conditioned Stimulus (CS)—Added agent.
-   Conditioned Response (CR)—New association that is learned.

*Other principles of CC:*
-   Counter-conditioning: The attempt to condition the subject to a different stimulus that will elicit a different response.
-   Avoidance Conditioning: Where the subject is taught to avoid a certain type of stimulus.
-   Extinction: When the conditioned stimulus/response (CS/CR) goes away without the presence of an unconditioned stimulus (UCS).
-   Spontaneous Recovery: The reappearance of the conditioned response (CR) with/without reinforcement after extinction has occurred.
-   Reinforcement (CC): Presenting the unconditioned stimulus (UCS) immediately after the conditioned stimulus/response (CS/CR).
-   Intermittent Reinforcement: Occasional reinforcement.
-   Generalization: When other "similar" stimulus will bring about a learned response.
-   Discrimination: By responding to a particular stimulus in one way and to a similar stimulus in another way.

## Operant Conditioning:

-   The type of learning where the strengthening of a stimulus-response relationship will occur when it is followed by a reinforcement.
-   Standard practice used in teaching/school
-   Extinction and Spontaneous Recovery will also occur with OC

- Generalization and Discrimination will also be part of Operant learning
- Where Ivan Pavlov is mainly associated with Classical Conditioning, *B.F. Skinner* has a similar association with Operant Conditioning.

*"Shaping"*—A term used with Skinnerian study, it states that when you reward the organism when it makes the correct response (or close to the desired response), it will create learning. "Skinner Box".

*Positive(or Primary) Reinforcement*—Usually considered a reward, and will strengthen a response.

*Negative Reinforcement*—This will strengthen the response by the absence of a reinforcement.

*Punishment*—A negative stimulus after undesirable behavior has occurred.

*Intermittent Reinforcement* (2 types):
1. Ratio Schedule: Depends on the *number* of correct responses between reinforcement.
   -Fixed ratio
   -Variable ratio
2. Interval Schedules: Utilizes the *time* between responses.
   -Fixed interval
   -Variable interval

*Secondary Reinforcement*—When a stimulus is *associated* with something that satisfies a need.

*\*Differences* between Classical Conditioning and Operant Conditioning:
- Subject takes a more active role in Operant
- Unconditioned Stimulus (UCS) is specifically known in Classical
- Reinforcer comes after the response in Operant

**Classical: Stimulus.........Reinforcement.........Response**
*Operant: Stimulus.........Response..........Reinforcement*

Also: "Social Learning" or "Model Learning" created by Albert Bandura.

**Other Types of Learning:**

*Programmed Learning*—Actually a type of Operant Conditioning that has had more recent success in the field of instruction. Involves the use of "Frames" which are a series of small steps that are presented to the learner to facilitate better learning.

1. <u>Linear Programs</u>: This uses a step-by-step, in-line process where the learner is taken through the material in a more organized fashion.
2. <u>Branching Programs</u>: Learner is allowed to proceed to another series of frames once they give the correct response or answer.

Biofeedback—The process of learning where the subject voluntarily regulates their body's response. Has been successfully used in treating headaches, high blood pressure/heart conditions, and hyperactivity.

*Cognitive Learning* (also known as Schakter's Principle)—In this type of learning you organize information, make comparisons, and form associations to assist in the learning process.

- Guided by past and present rewards and experiences and future expectations.
- E.C. Tolman was one of the innovators to this type learning and is credited with what he referred to as the <u>"Cognitive Map"</u>, where other situations and experiences can lead to understanding new events or situations.

*Edward Chace Tolman*

*Insight—The relatively sudden change in one's perception of a problem that results in the conclusion. Sometimes referred to as the "aha experience" or "the light goes on…".

# Chapter 10

## Learning, Remembering, and Forgetting

**Factors Affecting Learning:**

1. *Transfer*—The effect of previous learning on later learning, or later performance.

    - Positive Transfer: Improvement based on earlier learning
    - Negative Transfer: Earlier learning interferes with new learning

2. *Meaningfulness*—The rule that more meaningful information is learned more easily than nonsense.

3. *Feedback*—When you receive knowledge of the results of your learning effort.

4. *Massed and Distributed Practice* :

    - Massed: Running together of practice sessions
    - Distributed: Sessions are separated by rest periods

5. *Whole and Part Learning*:

    - Whole: Learning everything all at once
    - Part: Breaking learning down into smaller parts

6. *Mnemonic Devices*—Memory aids

- Catchwords
- Jingles
- Formulas
- Loci Method

7. *Overlearning*—Learning beyond a single, correct recitation.

8. *Chunking*—Combining or grouping of information into related groups.

**Progress of Learning:**

*Learning Curve*—A graph or concept of learning where the subject starts out slow, speeds up, then slows down again.

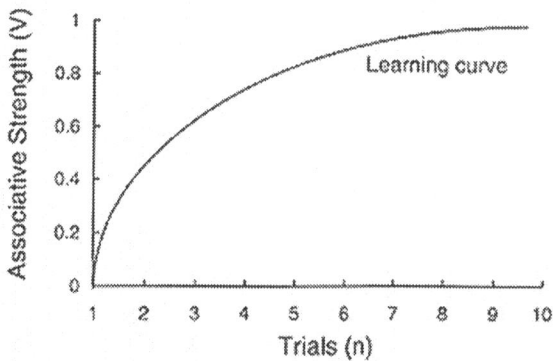

*Plateau*—A period during learning when little or no progress seems to be taking place. There are a number of reasons why this might take place, but the two most common are being bored or needing a better learning method or work method.

Remembering or Retention: 3 Methods…

1. *Relearning*—Things learned previously can be relearned with less effort.
2. *Recall*—Reproducing the material you've learned in the past.
3. *Recognition*—Ability to identify the answer, or something learned.

*Sleep and Remembering*—The old "wives tale" that you can learn while sleeping is not true. However, we do seem to remember things during level 1 or light sleep. Also, information is retained better when followed by rest.

**Memory:** 4 Processes

1. *Encoding*—When we change data from one system of communication to another.
2. *Rehearsal*—Memory becomes stronger when we repeat or practice that information.
3. *Storage*—If done properly, encoded and rehearsed information will be kept in your memory.
4. *Retrieval*—The actual process of recalling the information.

*The 3 Types or Parts of Memory:*

-    <u>Sensory Registers</u>: Information stored only momentarily
-    <u>Short-term Memory</u>: Stored for only a few seconds and has a limited capacity
-    <u>Long-term Memory</u>: More or less a permanent type of storage

*There is also a type of memory called *"episodic"* memory where you recall very important things that occurred in your past.

**Forgetting:** 5 Theories on why we forget…

1. *Elapse of time*—The brain will do a "memory trace" for information, but some will fade with time.
2. *Inattention*—Means you probably didn't have good concentration when you were learning the material.
3. *Retroactive inhibition*—New learning may interfere with the old learning.

4.  *Proactive inhibition*—The old learning interferes with the attempt at new learning.
5.  *Motivated forgetting*—There is a reason you will try to forget something or it will be done without your control.

# Chapter 11

## Thinking

*Thinking*—Unobservable activity by which a person or animal reorganizes past experiences through the use of symbols and concepts.

- Symbols: An object, act, or sound that stands for something else
- Concepts: The meaning that we attach to the qualities or characteristics that different objects, situations, or events have in common.

*Piaget's Theory on Thought Process:*

- Assimilation: When we take in new experiences and relate them to our existing cognitive structure.
- Accommodation: Changing our cognitive structure to adapt to each new experience.

*Uncritical Thinking*—The idea that your affiliations are the best, regardless of the facts. *Note: In childhood they tend to think in a very egocentric way, and as we mature we allow ourselves to become more open-minded.

- "All-or-Nothing" Thinking: Everything is either black or white, with little to no middle ground.
- Coincidence: The thought that because two things happen together, they may have caused each other.

- Delusions: A false belief that continues despite evidence to the contrary.

*Creative Thinking*—Allowing ourselves to discover new solutions to problems, or new ways of artistic expressions that are socially beneficial.

*Steps in the Creative Process:*
1. Preparation—The longest of the 4, sometimes referred to as the "soaking-up" process.
2. "Sitting on the Problem"—Putting the work away for awhile and maybe get away from it by doing something else.
3. Inspiration—When you get a sudden solution or idea associated with the problem.
4. Verification and Revision—Go back over the material again and make the changes and corrections as needed.

*Brainstorming*—A process where you, or a group attempt to solve a problem by expressing all the possible solutions, without evaluation or judgement.

*Measuring Creativity*—Although not a perfect science, there are a few ways that you can get an idea of someone who might be considered creative…

1. Incomplete Figure Test—Subject is given parts of a figure and they complete it.
2. Circles Task—They are given 36 circles and in a given amount of time they use them to create images.
3. Consequences—Usually your start with a statement like "What would happen if…", and they complete the thought a short story.
4. Imaginative Story—A little like the above, but they are given a theme and you would evaluate the story they create.

*Imagining*—These would be the pictures, images, and sounds that develop in our minds.

- Eidetic Images: The images become very lifelike and detailed in our minds, sometimes referred to as a "photographic memory".
- Imagination: How we reorganize and reproduce past experiences into a present idea. Similar to "fantasy".

*Problem Solving*—This will usually involve a goal that will incorporate the thinking process. Here are a few of the problem solving limitations and techniques that come into play when we try to solve problems.

1. *Functional fixedness*—Could be a hindrance when we become too focused or fixated on only one function or solution.
2. *Divergent thinking*—When we allow for flexibility or open-mindedness in our thinking.
3. *Reasoning*—The ability to comprehend or think in an orderly and rational way.
   - Inductive reasoning: When specific cases lead to general principles.
   - Deductive reasoning: When the general principles lead us to a specific case or consequence.

# Appendix B:

## Handwriting Analysis
### (Also referred to as Graphology or Graphoanalysis)

*Note: Use this as a "guide" to evaluate the handwriting you are trying to analyze. Remember, it must be writing and not printing to do a proper analysis.

### Analysis #1: Slant

Use your Emotional Expression Chart to measure the "*UP-strokes*" of the writing. This will measure the sample's emotional responsiveness or expression.

Slants from A to B:   Judgment will rule.
  Handles emergencies well.
  Not much emotional reaction.
  Uses the Head vs. the Heart.

Slants from B to C:   Quick to respond.
  Sympathetic
  Usually acts with thought.

Slants from C to D:   Very expressive.
  Emotional speakers.
  Acts quickly, often on impulses and without thought.

Slants from D to E:   Extremely emotional.
  Would make good salespersons, actors, writers, etc.

Slants from, or to the Left: *Note - lefthanders mostly slant the same as righties.
  Opposite of emotional expression
  Introverted and judgmental.

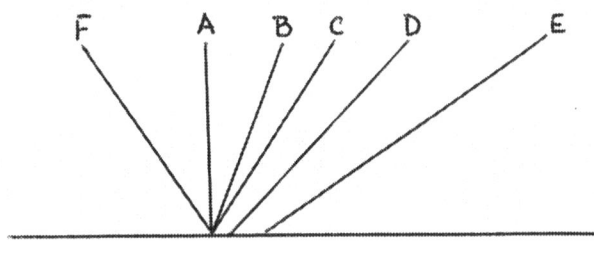

103

**Analysis #2: Type of Thinker**

1. *Exceptional Comprehension* (learning comes easy, may not feel the need to study):
   - Sharp, needle-like points (comprehension increases with the length of the point.)
   - Look for this in the lower case letters "m", "n", "r", and "s".
   - Said to have sharp, penetrating minds.

2. *Inquisitive:*
   - Enjoys learning. Wants to find out "why". Asks questions.
   - Explores, seeks knowledge, eager to dig-out facts.
   - Look for a rounded look (like an h that looks like an upside-down y).

   - Look for this in the lower case letters "m", "h", or "n".

3. *Non-thinkers* (have to work hard to achieve):
   - <u>Not</u> an indicator of intelligence however..
   - May not have an appreciation for learning and doing.
   - Look for illegible handwriting.

**Analysis #3: Appearance**

- Messy writing - messy mind. Tidy writing - tidy mind...
- Beauty of writing has nothing to do with personality.

**Analysis #4: Margins**

- Even: Tidy with an artistic eye.
- Narrow Left Margin: Reserved and hypersensitive.
- Narrow Right Margin: Generous or reckless. "Lives on the edge"
- Full Page: Has a lot to say or angry.
- Large Margins: Fearful, repressed, and fastidious personality.
- Strange, Ragged Left Margin: Insane, or temporary insanity.

**Analysis #5: Direction**

- Wanders Upward: Optimistic and healthy.
- Wanders Downward: Ill, mentally ill, pessimistic, or fatigued.
- Each word goes upward: Happy
- Each word goes downward: Unhappy

**Analysis #6: Spacing**

- Space between words is wide: Keeps others at a distance. *I hate you*
- Words are very close together: Possessive, clinging, or hostile. *I hate you*

## Analysis #7: Shape of Writing

- Wide Writing: Active and outgoing. *outdoors*
- Small Writing: Appreciates short, good work. Thrifty *small*
- Square Writing: Analytical, logical, a "mathematical" type. *math*
- Round Writing: Sociable, loving, and broad-minded. *round*
- Large Loops in Writing: Loves physical activity, athletic. *play*

## Analysis #8: Zones

- Upper Zone: Dreamer, ambitious, spiritual person.
- Middle Zone: Lives life day-to-day; focus is on social life, relationships, school, work, etc.
- Lower Zone: More "earthy" and physical needs (sex drive, materialism)

## Analysis #9: Capital Letters

- Large Capitals: Big ego *We are the best!*
- Small Capitals: Small ego *we are bad.*
- Ornamented Capitals: Vain or unusual personality. *Love*
- Leans to the side (more than other writing): Aggressive, fussy. *Play Ball*

## Analysis #10: Signatures

- Clear and Readable: Honest and open.
- Illegible: Shy or hiding something.
- Forename is Larger: Wants to be friendly or personal. *Bob Jones*
- Surname is Larger: Wants to keep things formal. *Bob Jones*
- A "Dot" after the Name: Tidy, or need to impress.
- Line Below Signature: Self-importance *Larry*
- Frilly or Twirls: Wants attention or wants to show their importance. *Sally*
- Line leading to Signature: Clings to the past *Bill*
- Line away from the Signature: Tactful, kind, and generous. *Joe*
- Placed in the Middle or Left of Page: Shy, introverted
- Placed on the Right: Cheerful and outgoing

**Analysis #11: The Letter "I"**

- Capital "I":
    + Large: Self-importance or opinionated. *I am the best*

    + Small: Low self-esteem. *Im terrible at this*

- Lower Case "I":
    + An "I-dot" centered means precision and concentration. *i or i*

    + Big "I-dots" might be showmanship tendencies. *i*

**Analysis #12: The Lower Case Letter "t":**

- Tells you more about the person than any other letter.
- Can apply to the letter "d" also.
- Look at the "stem" and "crossbar" (explained below...)

*Stem:*

- The taller it is the more is shows pride and vanity. *t*

- The shorter it is will show the opposite, but might mean they *t*
    are independent thinkers.

- "Loops" show sensitivity, easily hurt, and feel slighted sometimes. *t*

*Crossbars:*

- A "heavy" bar shows purpose, will-power, and determination. *t*

- Light bar shows lack of commitment and less force.

- "Levels": A 1 might undersell themselves        4 *t*
        A 4 has purpose and goals.                1 *t*

- A bar that is "arrow-like" to the right means temper, and
    if it is not connected to the stem is means an    *t or t*
    explosive temper.

- To the "left", procrastinates or hard to provoke. *t*

**Analysis #12 Cont.:**

*Crossbars:*

- Heavy arrow-like bar slanted downward: Demanding

- "Upside-down" Plates: Indicates self-control
    *Upward plate would be the opposite...

- Short "t-bars": Precision, no waste.

**"Other" Analysis to Consider:**

- Heavy down strokes in writing shows *determination* also.
- Long underlining of words shows *self-reliance* and self-confidence.
- "Hooks" could mean a desire to possess or be *possessive*.
- "Muddy" or blotchy writing should warn you of a sex criminal or someone with an *abnormal sex drive*.
- Small, squared loops at the end of "y", "g", or "j" *might* indicate a homosexual
    tendency.
- Large loops at the end of above letters indicates endowment, small loops not so much...

# Unit V

## Influencing Factors

# Chapter 12

## Sensation and Perception

*Sensation*—When we experience an arousal of one of our sense organs by something in the environment.

*Thresholds:*

1.   Absolute Threshold—The minimum amount of stimulus that a subject can detect through our sense organs.
2.   Difference Threshold—The amount of change in sensation needed for a subject to notice the difference.
3.   Just-noticeable Difference—Ability to distinguish between two stimuli that are seemingly close together.

*Perception*—How we interpret these sensations.

*Subliminal Perception*—When sensations are aroused by stimuli that are too weak for us to actually say we experienced it.

*Attention*—The process of focusing you perception on a limited number of stimuli.

-   The "stimuli": The intensity, size, contrast, movement, changes, novelty, and repetition that can all result in our paying more attention.

- The "individual": The condition of the individual like their needs, attitudes, expectations, motives, and past experiences that will be important factors in what is paid attention to.

*Perceiving Distance and Depth:*

- Convergence: The movement of the eye muscles causing the pupils to come closer together as an object is brought closer to the eyes.
- Texture Gradient: The amount of detail we are able to perceive in an object. Generally, the more detail we see, the closer it is.
- Linear Perspective: The further away objects are the closer together they seem to be.
- Atmospheric Perspective: Objects that are blurred by the atmosphere (fog, rain, etc.) will seem further away.

*Perception Patterns:*

- Proximity: Our tendency to group things together that are close to one another.

a.   Rule of proximity:
   Tendency to "put together" elements that are the clos-
   est together.

```
O O O O      O  O  O  O        O    O    O    O
O O O O      O  O  O  O        O    O    O    O
O O O O      O  O  O  O        O    O    O    O
```

-   Similarity: Grouping things together that resemble each other

a.   Rule of resemblance:
   Tendency to "put together" elements that are similar or
   that are repeated.

```
X O X O      XXXXXXX
X O X O      OOOOOO
X O X O      XXXXXXX
X O X O      OOOOOO
```

-   Closure: When the brain fills in the gaps to make an object
   complete or make sense of what we see.

a.   Rule of closure:
   Tendency to complete the missing parts of an object.

```
        A
    12 B 14
        C
```

*Optical Illusions*—A false visual perspective.

-   Practical uses for optical illusions:
   1.   Clothing—Horizontal stripes will make you look shorter
      and wider. Vertical stripes will make you look taller and
      thinner. Light colors will make you look thicker and
      larger, while dark colors will you look smaller.
   2.   Filmmaking and "flash cards"
   3.   Magical illusions

# Chapter 13

## Motivation and Emotion

**Motivation**—The activating of a behavior that will satisfy our needs and lead toward achievement of our goals.

> *Motives*—Specific expectations that cause us to strive toward a goal.

*Biological Drives:*

> *Drive*—A physiological condition that activates our behavior toward a goal.

- Hunger Drive: Seems to be controlled by the hypothalamus in the brain and also a "time" factor. Senses like taste, sight, and smell can also trigger this drive.
- Thirst Drive: Two widely accepted theories on thirst relate to the salt concentration and fluid levels in our bodies.

*Social Motives:*

- Achievement Motive: The need for, and the desire to succeed.
- Exploratory Motive: Our inborn curiosity that drives us to go places and do things formerly not experienced.
- Approval Motive: The need for the approval of others

*Intrinsic Motivation*—When we engage in activities simply because you enjoy them. Motivation that comes from within…

*Extrinsic Motivation*—We do things because of some external reward.

**Emotion**—Very often emotion is linked by a cause-and-effect relation-ship to motivation. This is a very complex state of awareness that involves bodily activity as well.

*Theories of Emotion:*

1. James-Lange Theory—Their theory was that emotions are the awareness of bodily changes that are occurring. James believed that these were primarily visceral reactions, while Lange would add that there is a vascular reaction as well.

2. Cannon-Bard Theory—They believed that our "awareness" of emotions and the body changes occur at the same time.

3. Cognitive Theory—In this theory, the mental process has to be involved in our emotional responses and experiences.

*Ways of measuring Emotion:*

- Breathing
- Heartbeat
- Galvanic Skin Response (GSR)
- Changes in the pupil of the eye
- Polygraph or lie detector (*Uses the subject's blood pressure, pulse, breathing, and GSR). Considered to be about 75% effective…

## Polygraph

# Chapter 14

## Frustration and Conflict

**Frustration**—What we experience whenever goal-directed activities are slowed-up, made difficult, or become impossible.

> *Frustration tolerance*—The level to which we are able to deal with these frustrations without becoming maladjusted or overly upset.

*Causes of Frustration:*
1. Motive (could be biological or social)
2. Several frustrating events in a short amount of time
3. Emotional stability of the individual
4. Distance from the goal
   - <u>Approach gradient</u>: How the strength of our frustration <u>increase</u>s the nearer we get to an attractive goal and not achieve it.
   - <u>Avoidance gradient</u>: How the frustration seems to <u>decrease</u> a little as we get further away from an undesirable situation.

**Conflict**—When we have to choose between alternatives or two possibilities.

> - *Approach-Approach Conflict*: When two situations or choices arise and you like both, but you have to choose between the two.

- *Avoidance-Avoidance Conflict*: When you are faced with two alternatives that are both unattractive but have to decide on one.
- *Approach-Avoidance Conflict*: Situations in which you are drawn toward certain aspects of a situation, but do not like other aspects.

**Adjustment Mechanisms**—These are the ways we behave that help to satisfy a need, reduce anxiety from frustration, or protect the individual's self-esteem.

1. *Compensation*—The attempt to make-up for a lack in one area by putting forth extra effort and energy over an extended period to do well in some other area. Some compensation techniques can be good, but others can be viewed as bad by society.

2. *Overcompensation*—Like compensation, but now you are going even further than just balancing their feelings of inferiority, guilt, frustration, or inadequacy.

3. *Identification*—The process of coping or associating closely with the behavior of other individuals or groups.

4. *Projection*—When we perceive our own undesirable traits or motives in other people.

5. *Stereotyping*—The act of continuing in a blind way with past behavior patterns and attitudes with no desire to change with the circumstances or current mores of society.

6. *Repression*—Sometimes referred to as "selective forgetting", this is where we forget because the original thought are too painful. A similar type of adjustment is called Suppression (or "motivated forgetting) where we try to forget a painful experience.

7. *Regression*—When we return to earlier ways of behaving to avoid present problems or our inability to deal with our frustrations.

8.  *Procrastination*—A very common trait where we try to escape problems by delaying or putting off a task.

9.  *Displaced aggression*—The transferring of anger or aggression from one source of frustration to some less threatening person or object.

10. *Rationalization*—Using socially approved reasons, instead of real reasons to explain their behavior. Also to blame an object or set of circumstances for your problems, failure, or guilt.

11. *Scapegoat*—When an individual or group is blamed for the misdeeds or mistakes of others.

12. *Sublimation*—Where we channel our impulses into more socially acceptable behavior.

13. *Denial*—Refusing to accept reality.

14. *Reaction Formation*—Reverses an unacceptable impulse and keeps it at the unconscious level.

# Unit VI

## Abnormal Psychology

# Chapter 15

## Stress

*Stress*—The body's reaction to perceived pressures and threats from the environment.

*Stress can be experienced on many different levels. It can be felt on a *Physical* level with an accelerated heart rate, increased blood pressure, the "shakes", stomach problems, headaches, etc. On a *Behavioral* level a person might smoke, take medications and drugs, bite their nails, etc. And finally it can be experienced on a *Psychological* level where it can turn into a mental illness or a mental breakdown (discussed more in Chapt. 16).

*Stressors*—These are the causes of stress. They can be:

- Positive (eustress) or Negative (distress)
- Physical or Psychological
- Short term or Long term

*"Fight or Flight" Reaction*—A phrase first coined by Dr. Walter Cannon in 1920 to describe how at moments of stress our choice might be to fight the stress that is present or run away from it.

*General Adaptation Syndrome (GAS)*—This syndrome is how we generally react to a stressful situation and occurs in 3 stages:

1.  <u>Alarm</u> (fight or flight)
2.  <u>Resistance</u> (try to maintain normalcy)
3.  <u>Exhaustion</u> (need for rest, or breakdown)

Things that can determine Stress:

1.  <u>Personality</u>—The stability of the individual is important, and whether they have a Type A or B personality will also be a factor.
2.  <u>Expectations</u>—Predictability generally will reduce stress
3.  <u>Degree of Control</u>—Refers to how much control we have over a situation.
4.  <u>Amount of Responsibility</u>—Generally the positive correlation is that the more responsibility we get the more the stress level rises.
5.  <u>Amount of Information</u>—The more information we have will usually help to reduce the amount of stress we experience.

*Change*—As a stressor it is generally considered the <u>number 1</u> cause of stress. Reasons for this could be because of the *<u>unpredictable</u>* nature of certain changes, the *<u>lack of control</u>* we sometimes have with the change, the *increased responsibility* that also goes with some changes, and that there is often *less information* that goes with the change.

*Stress Experiences:*
- Major Life Changes (death, divorce, changing jobs, moving, etc.)

   *Holmes and Rabe developed a Social Readjustment Rating Scale (SRRS) that assigns points to a list of major life changes. By adding up the points on this scale it would give you the possibility of becoming ill with a stress-related illness:
   
   Over 300 points—90% chance
   
   150 to 300—A 50-50 chance
   
   Less than 150—A 1 in 3 chance

| | |
|---|---:|
| Death of a Spouse | 100 |
| Divorce | 73 |
| Marital separation from mate | 65 |
| Detention in jail/other institution | 63 |
| Death of a close family member | 63 |
| Major personal injury or illness | 53 |
| Marriage | 50 |
| Being fired at work | 47 |
| Marital reconciliation with mate | 45 |
| Retirement from work | 45 |
| Major change in health/behavior of a family member | 44 |
| Pregnancy | 40 |
| Sexual difficulties | 39 |
| Gaining a new family member | 39 |
| Major business readjustment | 39 |
| Major change in financial state | 38 |
| Death of a close friend | 37 |
| Changing to a different line of work | 36 |
| Major change in number of arguments with spouse (a lot more or a lot less) | 35 |
| Taking out a mortgage or loan for a major purchase | 31 |

| | |
|---|---|
| Foreclosure on a loan | 30 |
| Major change in responsibilities at work (promotion, demotion, transfer) | 29 |
| Son or daughter leaving home | 29 |
| In-law troubles | 29 |
| Outstanding personal achievement | 28 |
| Wife beginning or ceasing work outside the home | 26 |
| Beginning or ceasing formal schooling | 26 |
| Major change in living conditions (i.e. building new home, remodeling) | 25 |
| Revision of personal habits (dress, manners, association, etc) | 24 |
| Troubles with the boss | 23 |
| Major change in working hours or condition | 20 |
| Change in residence | 20 |
| Changing to a new school | 20 |
| Major change in type/amount of recreation | 19 |
| Major change in church activities | 19 |
| Major change in social activities | 18 |
| Taking out a mortgage or loan for lesser purchase | 17 |
| Major change in sleeping habits | 16 |
| Major change in family get-togethers | 15 |
| Major change in eating habits | 15 |
| Vacation | 13 |
| Christmas | 12 |
| Minor violations of the law (traffic tickets, jaywalking, disturbing the peace) | 11 |

-    Daily Hassles (the little things that occur day-to-day that contribute to the overall stress we experience)

*Stress Through the Life Cycles*—These are the major contributors to the stress in our lives based on your age group.

-    Infancy and Childhood: Empty stomach, wet diaper, lack of sleep, boredom, lack of stimulation, and school.

- <u>Adolescence</u> (most stressful time): Body changes, independence struggles, dating, college, and careers.
- <u>Adulthood</u>: Marriage, independence, increased responsibility, children, and work.
- <u>Later Adulthood</u>: Being alone, loss of energy, poor health, and possible loss of a spouse.

*Ways of Controlling Stress:*

- <u>Getting away from the stressor</u> (take a break, go on vacation, walk away, etc.)
- <u>Biofeedback techniques</u> (deep breathing, counting to 10, etc.)
- <u>Medications</u> (prescribed and illegal)
- <u>Exercise</u> (works to take your mind off of the stress and also strengthens the body to better handle the stress)
- <u>Social Support System</u> (people in our lives that can help us in a stressful time)
- <u>Relaxation techniques</u> (meditation, music, videotapes, etc.)

# Chapter 16

## Psychological Disorders

In this lengthy chapter we will take an in-depth look at the various categories of mental disorders (in no particular order) along with their types and subtypes that are defined in the Diagnostic and Statistical Manual of Mental Disorders-Fourth Edition (with Text Revision), or DSM-IV TR (formerly DSM IV).

*Abnormal Behavior*—This has long been one of the most difficult areas to define. What is normal? It takes the long studied knowledge of the psychiatric profession to help us sort out what behavior might be noticeably different or abnormal. Two types of abnormal behavior could be classified as:

- Neurosis: Somewhat mild and common disturbances that involve an element of either anxiety, mild depression, personality peculiarities, or other less severe disturbances.

- Psychosis: Those with the inability to cope with, or distinguish from reality. They could also be of harm to themselves or others if untreated.

## Psychological Disorders

Schizophrenia—Disorder characterized by distortions of reality, disturbances in emotions and thought, strange behavior, and confusion as to identity or time.

- Always involves delusions, hallucinations, or disturbances in affective thought.
- Presence of a family pattern.
- Occurs usually early in adult life.
- Shows up in disturbances in work, social relations, and self care.

**Delusions**—A belief that persists in spite of evidence or proof to the contrary.

- Delusions of Persecution (ex. Someone is out to hurt them)
- Delusions of Reference (ex. The world revolves around them)
- Delusions of Grandeur (ex. They believe they are someone important)

*Other less frequent delusions:
  - "Thought Broadcasting"
  - "Thought Insertion"
  - "Thought Withdrawal"
  - Being Controlled

**Hallucinations**—Usually a "sensory" type of misperception.

- Tactile (electrical tingling or burning sensation)
- Somatic (body sensation)
- Visual, Gustatory (taste), or Olfactory (smell)
- Auditory (hearing) *Most common type…

*Symptoms:*

- Isolation or withdrawal
- Impaired role-function
- Peculiar behavior
- Impaired hygiene and grooming
- Odd beliefs or Magical thinking
- Sensing the presence of a force or person not there
- Lack of motivation

*Some Subtypes of Schizophrenia:*

**Catatonic Type:** Psychomotor disturbance.
-   Stupor
-   Negativism
-   Rigidity
-   Excitement
-   Posturing

**Disorganized Type:** Incoherent, has inappropriate behavior, and losses past associations.

**Paranoid Type:** Unfocused anxiety, anger, and violence. Frequently argumentative and often has hallucinations (auditory usually) of a single theme.

**Anxiety Disorders**—Several categories of disorders that create difficulties in dealing with everyday life experiences.

**1. Panic Disorder**—Features recurrent panic attacks with periods of intense fear or discomfort. Sometimes referred to as a "panic attack".

- Usually lasts anywhere from a few minutes to several hours.
- Can come on unexpectedly.
- Person can feel intense apprehension, fear, terror, or even doom.
- Onset is usually in the late 20's.
- Equally common in males and females.
- Can sometimes be initiated by stimulant drugs.

*Symptoms*: (*Must show at least 4 for a diagnosis)

| | |
|---|---|
| -Shortness of breath | -Dizziness |
| -Smothering sensation | -Faintness |
| -Unsteady feelings | -Choking |
| -Accelerated heart-rate | -Trembling/shaking |
| -Abdominal distress | -Sweating |
| -Numbness or tingling | -Nausea |
| -Hot flashes | -Chills |
| -Chest pains | -Fear of dying |

**2. *Agoraphobia*—**Fear of being in places or situations from which escape might be perceived as difficult. (*Often associated with Panic Disorder/Attacks)

- Can restrict a person's travel.
- Needs a "companion" when away from home.
- May be triggered by being outside alone, in a crowd, standing in line, crossing a bridge, or traveling in a bus/train/car.
- Begins in the 20's or 30's and can last for years.
- By far more common in females.

*Symptoms:*
- Becomes dizzy or falls.
- Loses bladder control.

- Vomits
- Has cardiac distress.

**3. Social Phobia**—Persistent fear of being scrutinized by others and doing something humiliating or embarrassing.

- Fear of public speaking, or saying something foolish.
- Choking on food in front of others.
- Unable to urinate in a public restroom.
- Begins in Childhood.
- More common in males.

*Symptoms:*
- Stuttering
- Trembling
- Abnormal eating behavior
- Panic and sweating
- Tachycardia (fast heartbeat) and difficulty breathing

**4. Specific Phobia (formerly known as Simple Phobia)**—Fear of objects or situations that usually leads to humiliation or embarrassment.

Most Common at certain ages…

- Dogs, snakes, mice, bugs, etc. (Childhood)
- Blood/Injury (Adolescence) *chance of fainting…
- Claustrophobia (Adulthood) *closed in spaces
- Acrophobia (Adulthood) *heights
- Aerophobia (Adulthood) *air travel/flying

Types:

- Animal (includes insects)
- Natural Environment (water, storms, heights, etc.)
- Situational (flying, tunnels, bridges, etc.)

*Simple phobias are more common in females.

**5. Obsessive-Compulsive Disorder (OCD)**—Recurrent obsessions and/or compulsions severe enough to cause distress, become time-consuming, or interfere with a person's routine, occupation, social activities, or relationships.

**Obsessions**—Ideas, thoughts, impulses, or images that are intrusive and senseless.
*Most Common:*
- Thoughts of violence
- Contamination
- Doubt

**Compulsions**—Repetitive, purposeful, and intentional behaviors that are performed in response to an obsession.

*Most Common:*
- Hand-washing
- Counting
- Checking
- Touching

*Both sexes are equally affected by this disorder. Usually begins at adolescence or early adulthood.

**6. Post-Traumatic Stress Disorder (PTSD)**—Follows a psychologically distressing event that is outside the range of usual human experience.

- Usually experiences fear, terror, and a sense of helplessness.
- Onset can be at any age.
- Situations or activities "similar" to the original trauma can activate PTSD symptoms/

*Symptoms:* (*must have at least 2 for a diagnosis)
- Difficulty falling or staying asleep.
- Irritability or outbursts of anger.
- Difficulty concentrating.
- Hypervigilance and physiologic reactivity.
- Exaggerated startle response.

*Most common causes of PTSD:*
- Threats to one's life or physical integrity.
- Threats to harm one's children, spouse, or close relative/friend.
- Destruction of one's home or community.
- Seeing someone else killed or seriously injured.

*Early Names for PTSD:*
- "Railroad Heart" (1800's)
- "Soldier's Heart" (WWI)
- "Shell Shocked" (WWII)
- "Combat Fatigue" (WWII)
- "Battle Fatigue" (WWII)
- PTSD (60's and 70's—Vietnam)

**7. General Anxiety Disorder (GAD)**—Unrealistic or excessive anxiety and worry about two or more life circumstances.

*Symptoms:*
- Motor tension
- Autonomic hyperactivity
- Vigilance and Scanning

*Most common in a person's 20's or 30's and is equally common in males and females.

Also: **Acute Stress Disorder**—Experiences a sense of numbing, detachment, or absence of emotion. The traumatic event is persistently reexperienced.

**Somatoform Disorders**—Physical symptoms suggest a physical illness for which there is positive evidence, or a strong presumption that the symptoms are linked to a *psychological* factor or conflict.

- Conversion Disorder
- Hypochondriasis
- Body Dysmorphic Disorder (BDD)

**1. Conversion Disorder**—Alteration or loss of physical functioning that suggests physical problems, but is apparently psychological.

*Symptoms:*

| | |
|---|---|
| -Paralysis | -Seizures |
| -Blindness | -Coordination disturbance |
| -Tunnel Vision | -Vomiting |
| - False Pregnancy | |

*Other Aspects of the Disorder:*
- Onset is in early adulthood or adolescence
- Features extreme psychological stress
- Complicates normal life activities
- Most cases occur in wartime

**2. Hypochondriasis** (hypochondria/hypochondriac)—Preoccupation with fear of having, or the belief that one has, a serious disease.

*Symptoms:*
- Persists despite medical reassurance
- Preoccupation with body functions
- Preoccupation with a specific organ
- "Doctor Shopping"
- Refuses *mental* health care
- Can begin at any age, but most common in 20's and 30's
- Equally common in males and females

**3. Body Dysmorphic Disorder (or BDD)**—Preoccupation with some imagined defect in appearance—in a normal-appearing person.

*Common Complaints:*
- Facial Flaws (Wrinkles, Spots, Excess hair, etc.)
- Shape of Nose, Mouth, Jaw, or Eyebrows
- Other Body Parts like Feet, Hands, Breasts, Back, etc.

*Characteristics of the Disorder:*
- Repeated visits to Plastic Surgeons and Dermatologists
- Depression
- Avoidance/Withdrawal
- Onset usually from Adolescence through 30's

Also:

**Somatization Disorder**—Many complaints causing problems in social and occupational functioning.

**Pain Disorder**—Pain in one or more body locations.

*Mood Disorders (or Affective Disorders)*—Change in a prolonged emotion, generally involving either depression or elation.
   Parts:
-   Manic Episodes
-   Depressive Disorders
-   Symptoms

**Manic Episodes**—Predominant mood is either elation or irritability. Onset is in the early 20's or after age 50.

*Symptoms:*
-   Elevated Mood
-   Inflated Self-esteem
-   Decreased Need for Sleep
-   Manic Speech
-   Distractibility
-   Increase in Goal Directed Activities

**Depressive Episodes**—Depressed mood, loss of interest (or pleasure) in all, or almost all activities. Onset can be at any age, but most common in late 20's.

*Symptoms:*
-   Appetite disturbance
-   Change in weight
-   Sleep disturbance
-   Decreased energy
-   Feeling worthless
-   Guilt
-   Thoughts of death
-   Suicide (or attempts)

*Age-Specific Features:*
-   Prepubescent Children (Moody, body complaints, and hallucinations)
-   Adolescents (Antisocial, use of alcohol or drugs, aggression, grouchy, or withdrawn)

- Elderly Adults (Memory loss, loss of interest or pleasure, and inattentiveness)

**Bipolar Disorder** (formerly manic-depression)—One or more Manic episodes usually accompanied by one or more Depressive Episodes.

*Symptoms:*
- Characterized by rather large emotional swings
- Equally common in males and females
- Onset is usually from Adolescence to late 20's

**Other Mood Disorders:**

1. **Melancholy** (Melancholic Features Specifier)—Loss of pleasure in all, or almost all activities.

2. **Postpartum** (Postpartum Onset Specifier)—Onset within 4 weeks after the delivery of a child. Can have psychotic features.

3. **Seasonal Affective Disorder/SAD** (Seasonal Pattern Specifier)—
    Begins in the Fall and ends in the Spring. Women have 60-90% of cases.

**Dissociative Disorders**—Disturbance or alteration in the normal function of identity, memory, or consciousness.

- Multiple Personality Disorder (MPD/DID)
- Psychogenic Fugue
- Psychogenic Amnesia

**Multiple Personality Disorder** (now known as **Dissociative Identity Disorder** or DID)—Existence within the person of two or more distinct personalities or personality states.

*Symptoms or Characteristics:*
- At least two "fully" developed personalities
- Each has a unique memory, behavior, and social relationship
- Number of personalities varies from 2 to well over 100
- "Transitions" are triggered by:
  + Psychosocial stress
  + Conflicts
  + Hypnosis
- Each personality may differ in:
  + Psychological testing
  + Eyeglass prescriptions
  + Medications
  + IQ
  + Sex
  + Race or Age
  + Family background
- Most Personalities have:
  + Proper names (but all different)
  + Symbolic meanings
  + Function names
- Onset always in Childhood
- Three to Nine times more common in females
- Complications:
  + Suicide attempts
  + Self-mutilation

+   Child abuse
+   Assaults and Rapes

**Psychogenic Fugue**—Sudden unexpected *travel* away from home or work with a new identity and no recall of their previous identity.

*Symptoms or Characteristics:*
-   Usually becomes more outgoing and uninhibited than before
-   Takes up a new name, residence, and social activity
-   Heavy alcohol use may lead to this disorder
-   Follows severe psychological stress like…
    +   Marital quarrels
    +   Personal rejection
    +   Military conflict
    +   Natural disaster
-   Continues for many months
-   Travel can be over thousands of miles and even across national borders
-   Most common in Wartime, or in the wake of a Natural Disaster
-   Recovery is rapid, and recurrences are rare

**Psychogenic Amnesia**—Sudden inability to recall important personal information.

*Four Types of Amnesia:*
1.   Localized (*most common)—Failure to recall all events during a certain period of time.
2.   Selective—Failure to recall some, but not all events during a certain period of time.
3.   Generalized—Encompasses the person's entire life.
4.   Continuous—Cannot recall events after a specific time up to, and including the present.

Symptoms and Characteristics:
-   Perplexity
-   Disorientation

- Purposeless wandering
- PTSD may also be present
- In Females, the onset is usually in adolescence or early adulthood
- In Males, onset is more common in war
- Rare in the elderly
- Can be brought about by Severe Psychosocial Stress, Unacceptable impulses or acts, Threats of injury or death, and an Intolerable life situation.
- Termination is abrupt, recovery is usually complete, and reoccurrences are rare

**Sexual Disorders** (or Paraphilias/Sexual Deviations)—Sexual fantasies generally involving either (1) nonhuman objects, (2) the suffering or humiliation or one's self or others, or (3) children or other nonconsenting persons.

*Symptoms or Characteristics:*
-    "Para" means deviation, and "philia" means attracted to...
-    Always must be included in the sexual activity
-    Severity of disorder is based on acting on urges or not
-    Sex Ratios: 20 to 1 Males

*Most Common Activities:*
-    Excited by a particular fantasy (ex. Female undergarments)
-    Being humiliated
-    Being injurious to partner or self

*Types of displays:*
-    Having an occupation or hobby that brings contact
-    Working with children (volunteers)
-    Driving an ambulance or medical work
-    Collects "preferred" pornography
-    Pursues a "specific" stimulus
-    Purchases the services of someone to satisfy a fantasy
-    Acts out fantasies on an unwilling victim

**Types:**
-    Exhibitionism
-    Fetishism
-    Frotteurism
-    Pedophilia
-    Masochism
-    Sadism
-    Transvestism
-    Voyeurism

**Exhibitionism**—Disorder involving the exposure of one's genitals to a stranger.

*Symptoms and Characteristics:*
- Usually not physically dangerous
- Desire is to shock or surprise the observer
- Only in Males and victims are almost always women and children
- Age at onset is usually before age 18, and becomes less severe after 40

**Fetishism**—Disorder involving the use of nonliving objects (fetishes).

*Most Common "Objects":*
- Bras
- Women's underpants
- Stockings
- Shoes or boots
- Other wearing apparel

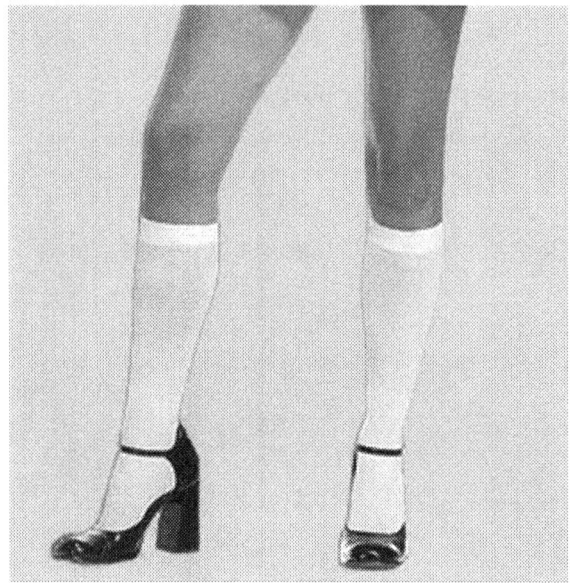

*Symptoms and Characteristics:*
- Begins usually by Adolescence
- Masturbation is usually involved while holding, rubbing, or smelling the object
- May also ask the partner to wear the object during a sexual encounter

**Frotteurism**—Disorder involving touching and rubbing against a non-concenting person.

*Symptoms and Characteristics:*
- Usually commits the "frottage" in crowded places
- While rubbing against, or fondling the victim they fantasize about having a caring relationship with them
- Begins in Adolescence

**Pedophilia**—Involves sexual activity with a prepubescent child.

*Symptoms and Characteristics:*
- If attracted to Girls, they prefer 8 to 10 year olds (x2)
- If attracted to Boys, they prefer 10 to 13 year olds
- Could be aroused by both sexes
- Those who "act" on their urges:
    + Undress the child and just look
    + Expose themselves
    + Masturbate in their presence
    + Touches and fondles
- May be limited to his own children, stepchildren, or relatives
- Threats usually made to prevent disclosure

*Techniques for obtaining their victims:*
- Winning the trust of the child's mother
- Marrying a woman with an attractive child
- Trading children with other pedophiles
- Obtaining a foster child
- Abduction

*Begins at adolescence, but not usually aroused until middle age.

**Masochism**—Involves the act of being humiliated, beaten, bound, or otherwise made to suffer. *Present in Childhood.

*Masochistic "Fantasies":*
- Being raped while being held down or bound
- Binding themselves
- Sticking themselves with pins
- Shocking themselves electrically
- Self-mutilation

*"Acts" with a Partner:*
- Restraint (called Physical Bondage)
- Blindfolding (Sensory Bondage)
- Paddling, spanking, whipping (Flagellation)
- Beating, electrical shocks, cutting, pinning, or piercing
- Humiliation
- Infantilism

*Most Dangerous: Hypoxyphilia (arousal by oxygen deprivation)
- Noose
- Plastic bag
- Mask
- Chemical
- Chest compression

**Sadism**—Involves acts in which psychological or physical suffering of the victim is sexually exciting.

*Symptoms and Characteristics:*
- Needs complete control over the victim, who is usually terrified
- Consenting partner is usually a Masochist
- Present in Childhood, but acted upon by early Adulthood

Typical Fantasies of the Sadist:
- Forcing the victim to crawl
- Blindfolding
- Keeping the victim in a cage
- Paddling
- Electrical shocks
- Spanking
- Cutting or stabbing
- Whipping
- Strangulation
- Pinching
- Torture
- Mutilation
- Beating
- Burning
- Rape
- Killing

**Transvestic Fetishism**—Disorder involving cross-dressing.

Symptoms and Characteristics:
- Usually involves a collection of women's clothing worn when alone
- Arousal occurs imagining other males being attracted to him as a woman
- Some may wear only a single item of women's clothing under their masculine attire
- Some may wear make-up and dress entirely as a woman
- Degree to which they appear as a woman depends on:
    + Mannerisms
    + Body habitus
    + Cross-dressing skills
- Onset is Childhood, but does not go public until Adulthood
- Some seek Surgical or Hormonal sex reassignment
- History shows cases of "petticoat punishment" as an early cause, but newer theories have replaced that notion

**Voyeurism**—Involves the act of observing unsuspected people, usually strangers, who are either naked, in the process of undressing, or engaging in sexual activity.

Symptoms and Characteristics:
- No sexual activity, only the act of "peeping"
- Fantasy of having a sexual experience with the "observed"
- Usually develops before age 15

**Other Sexual Disorders:**

- Telephone Scatologia (obscene caller)
- Necrophilia (corpses)
- Apotemnophilia (limb removal)
- Partialism (parts of the body)
- Zoophilia or Bestiality (animals)
- Coprophilia (feces)
- Klismaphilia (enemas)
- Urophilia (urine)

*Personality Disorders*—A continuing pattern of inner experience and behavior that deviates markedly from the expectations of the individual's culture.

*Paranoid Personality Disorder*—Pervasive distrust and suspiciousness of others such that their motives are interpreted as malevolent (ill will, hatred, etc.). Keyword—**paranoid**.

*Schizoid Personality Disorder*—Detachment from social relationships and a restricted range of expression of emotions in interpersonal settings. Keyword—**detached**.

*Schizotypal Personality Disorder*—Pattern of social and interpersonal deficits marked by acute discomfort with, and reduced capacity for close relationships as well as cognitive or perceptual distortions. Keyword—**eccentric**.

*Histrionic Personality Disorder*—Excessive emotion and attention seeking. Keyword—**theatrical**.

*Narcissistic Personality Disorder*—Pattern of grandiosity (fantasy or behavior) need for admiration, and lack of empathy. Keyword—**self-importance**.

*Antisocial Personality Disorder*—Disregard for, and violation of, the rights of others. Keywords—**frequent arrests**.

*Borderline Personality Disorder*—Instability of interpersonal relationships, self image, affect, and marked impulsivity. Keyword—**unstable**.

*Avoidant Personality Disorder*—Social inhibition, feelings of inadequacy, and hypersensitive to negative evaluation. Keyword—**shy**.

*Dependent Personality Disorder*—Pervasive and excessive need to be taken care of that leads to submissive clinging behavior and fears of separation. Keyword—**clinging**.

*Obsessive-Compulsive Personality Disorder*—Preoccupation with orderliness, perfectionism, mental/personal control, at the expense of flexibility, openness, and efficiency. Keyword—**perfectionism**.

# Chapter 17

## Treatment of Disorders

**Medical Therapies**—Physical treatment through medicine and surgery.

- *Drug Therapy*: Medicines used to aid in the treatment of mental disorders. Drug categories used would be things like tranquilizers, lithium, antipsychotics, psychotropics, etc.

- *Psychosurgery*: The use of brain surgery (e.g. lobotomy) to correct a mental condition.

- *Electroconvulsive Shock Therapy*: Shocking certain areas of the brain, usually for only a few seconds, to stimulate brain activity.

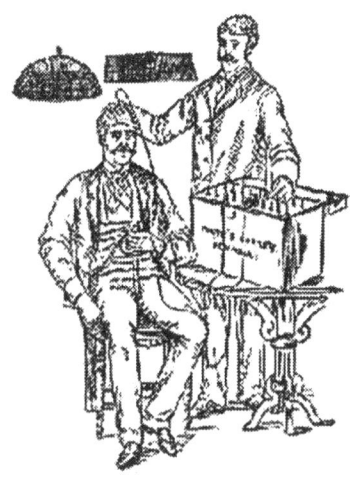

**Psychotherapy**—Interaction of the patient with a psychiatric professional.

- *Psychoanalysis*: A therapy to help the patient remember forgotten motives and experiences. If allowed to run to completion has been about 75% successful. The 4 types are generally:
  1. Dream Interpretation
  2. Free Association
  3. Resistance
  4. Transference

- *Play Therapy*: Done by observing and analyzing children at play
- *Client-centered Therapy*: Subjects are allowed to talk on their own and try to analyze problems with the aid of a therapist
- *Transactional Analysis* (TA): Used extensively in marriage and family counseling and utilizes a 3-part approach—Parent, Adult, and Child.

**Behavior Therapy**—Also sometimes referred to as Behavior Modification Therapy, it bases the focus on the actual behavior itself. The concept is that we have either learned inadequate ways of behaving, or that we cannot cope with everyday problems.

- *Aversive Therapy*: The attempt to change undesirable behavior by pairing it with a punishment.

### Smoking Cessation Programs: Aversion Therapy

Aversion therapy pairs the pleasurable stimulus of smoking a cigarette with some unpleasant stimulus. Perhaps the most common form of aversion therapy is rapid, or "quick puff" smoking, in which the smoker inhales frequently and consistently until reaching the point of nausea. Another form of aversion therapy, and one that is sometimes used at the same time as rapid smoking, involves brief electrical shocks at each step of the smoking process (opening the pack, pulling out a cigarette, bringing a cigarette toward the mouth, placing the cigarette between the lips, lighting it, and puffing the cigarette).

- *Desensitization*: The attempt to get rid of an undesirable response by strengthening the opposite response.

- *Implosive Therapy*: Where the patient experiences the anxiety provoking situation with the knowledge that there will be no harmful effects associated with the experiences.

- *Simple Extinction Therapy*: From the Behavioral school of psychology, the lack of a reward is practiced to try and eliminate a particular behavior.

- *Modeling*: The attempt to change a behavior by watching or imitating a behavior model.

**Group Therapy**—Therapies that deal with groups of people at the same time.

- *Encounter Groups*: Also known as T-Groups or Sensitivity Groups, it involves a group leader, about 10-15 people, and everyone interacts by expressing their feelings.

- *Family Therapy*: The attempt to help family members better understand the internal relationships. Sometimes a video recording is needed and one male and one female therapist to lead the group.

- *Psychodrama*: A therapy where the players act out their problems by playing roles in realistic situations.

**Mental Health Care Facilities**—Known by a variety of different names, there are some that deal with the "criminally" insane all the way down to those with only mild mental conditions.

- Once known as *Insane Asylums*, the treatment was often very cruel and inhumane. This was followed by treating patients similar to those with medical conditions and soon became known as *Mental Hospitals*.
- Facilities are now similar to *small communities* where patients are either residents or day-only clients. These facilities are often self-contained living environments offering work opportunities, recreation areas, entertainment features, and food services.

- Many of the changes that helped to bring about the current living conditions can be attributed to people like *Dorthea Dix* and *Clifford Beers*.

# Appendix C

## "The Violent Mind"
## (A Study of Criminal/Violent Behavior)

**Terms and Definitions:**

1. **Violence** (as it relates to mental illness...)—May involve hallucinations, delusions, and behavioral disturbances (ex. Cold, callous, casual attitude, and deliberate).

2. **Sociopath**—A person characterized by asocial or antisocial behavior.

3. **Psychopath**—A behavior disorder which is demonstrated in society in terms of criminal acts, drug addiction, sexual perversion, or immediate self-gratification without fear of punishment.

4. **Psychotic**—Out of touch with reality (also known as "moral insanity" and "psychopathic personality disorder".

   - 2 Forms of Psychosis: (1) treatable with medication as long as there are no recurrences and (2) Chronic, untreatable.
   - Can be: (1) *Biological*, like brain disease/head injury/body chemistry/etc. or (2) *Affective*, like temper/uncontrolled emotions/antisocial behavior/etc.

5.  **Criminology**—The scientific study of crime as a social phenomenon, criminal investigation, criminals, or the penal system/treatment.

6.  **The "Insanity Plea"**—To absolve from criminal responsibility for their action those persons who are incapable of exercising free and knowing choice of conduct.

7.  **Cannibalism**—The eating of flesh, organs, or eggs of any animal by its own kind.

8.  **Ritualistic Killing**—Carries out a murderous act in a prescribed or ritual-like fashion.

# Jack the Ripper
## (England—Late 1800's)

Facts:

- The identity is still unknown today. Those who continue to try and solve the mystery are known as "Ripperologists".
- Initially associated with killing "at least" 5 women during a 10 week period on the East end of London.
- Jack would slash the throat, disembowel the victim, and mutilate the bodies. Seemed to have a focus on the female sex organs.
- The murders were all prostitutes where in London there were 62 brothels and 233 hotels of ill-repute.
- Most famous of the victims was Mary Kelly because of her brutal and gruesome murder and the fact that she was several months pregnant.
- All the victims had left their families and turned to prostitution, which may have some relevance to why Jack committed the murders—"So was he in fact a murderer, or just an avenger?"
- He apparently had a good knowledge of post-mortem operations, which might indicate that he was a medical student or possibly even a doctor.
- He had written several letters to the authorities and Scotland Yard ridiculing them for their inability to catch him.
- There have been several similar cases thereafter, but many are believed to be just "copycats".

# Lizzie Borden
## (United States—1860–1927)

Facts:
- - Poem made famous:    Lizzie Borden took and axe, and gave
    her mother 40 whacks.
    And when she saw what she had done,
    She gave her father 41.

- She was a 32 year-old spinster who was "acquitted in her historic 1893 murder trial which all took place in Fall River, MA.

- Her mother and father (64 and 69 respectively), were found chopped to death with a hatchet.

- Actually it was her Step-mother who was hated by Lizzie for replacing her biological mother.

- Thoughts at the time were that she was worried about her inheritance.

- Others worried that it might be her father's business enemies who had threatened to burn the house down.

- There were many other suspects, including her sister Emma, that were under investigation but no one was ever convicted of the crime.

## Albert Fish
### (U.S.—1870-1936)

Facts:

- Raised in an orphanage in Washington D.C., where there was sadistic cruelty inflicted on the children.

- One author wrote that Albert "lived a life of unparalleled perversion".

- As the story goes, he just "snapped" one day in 1917 after his wife ran away with a lover.

- Some of his acts of perversion were:
    + Baying at the moon (naked), which was referred to as "moon mania".
    + Beating himself, or had others beat him until he bled.
    + Intentionally burning himself.
    + A known coprophiliac.
    + He was obsessed with cannibalism.
    + Also became a Sadist (killings and beatings).
    + Eventually became a pedophile.

- Eventually he was prosecuted for the death of 12 year-old Grace Budd, whom he decapitated, sawed in half, and made a stem from her flesh.

- During the first attempt to execute him (in the electric chair @ Sing-Sing prison), it failed due to all the needles he had inserted into his body. And although the second attempt was successful, it wasn't pretty…

- Before the execution he actually spoke of how he looked forward to it.

# Edward Gein
## (Plainfield, WI 1906–1984)

Facts:

- Named one of the most horrible killer-cannibals in U.S. history.
- Mother was a strong-willed woman who early on warned Eddy about the evils of women.
- Thought to be one of the models for the movie "Psycho".
- Would study human anatomy for many hours a day.
- Started out digging up bodies from graveyards where he would dissect and study them.
- Confessed that he "skinned" the corpses and wore it as clothing.
- He began murdering women in 1954. All the women had a striking resemblance to his mother.
- When he was eventually caught and his farmhouse searched, the sheriff of Portage County was unable to speak for hours after.
- There were numerous "trophies" found from approximately 15 women:
  + 4 noses in a cup
  + A bracelet made of human skins
  + A tom-tom made with a coffee can and human skin
  + A string of human lips
  + Table legs made from shinbones
  + Skin vests, stockings, and purse handles
  + Also, the famous "death masks"
- He also confessed to eating the flesh of some of the corpses.
- He died at Mendota Mental Hospital in 1984.

## Zodiac Killer
### (California, 1960's & 1970's)

Facts:

- Responsible for several killings in California, mostly preying on people in parked cars (mostly women).
- In his letters, he claimed to have killed 37 people and police estimate it could be anywhere from 6 to 40.
- Got the name by using the signs of the zodiac and cryptograms in his letters.
- The killings seemed to be his attempt to collect slaves for the after-life.
- He was never caught and there are still some attempts to identify him.
- Police believe he has either died, was committed to a psychiatric institution, or might have simply stopped killing.

## Albert DeSalvo
### (a.k.a. The Boston Strangler and The Measuring Man)
### Boston, MA 1931–1973

Facts:

- Believed to have sexually assaulted, then strangled at least 13 women between 1962 and 1964.

- His father was a tough, taskmaster who beat him over any little thing.

- Said he had an overactive sex drive which he claimed to need a minimum of 6 times a day.

- Called "The Measuring Man" because one of his tricks was to get himself invited to an attractive woman's apartment and take her measurements for a possible modeling job.

- Was diagnosed with Schizophrenia and kept in an asylum for several years.

- Was later transferred to Walpole State Prison where he was stabbed in the heart on Nov. 26, 1973.

## Charles Manson
### (a.k.a. Man-Son or Son-of-Man)
### California, 1931–

Facts:

- Was born the illegitimate son of a teenage prostitute.
- Spent most of his entire early life in and out of boy's homes and schools.
- By the time he was 33, he had spent 17 years in jail or in reformatories.
- His height (5'2"), might have been a possible factor as it contributed to his self-image.
- He seemed to have a hypnotic effect on women, especially those who sought out excitement.
- He also had an insatiable sex craving, which was obvious in the many "orgies" he had with his followers.
- He desperately hated black people, probably due to the many rapes he subjected to in prison.
- He did not actually commit the Tate/LaBianca murders, but he directed them in 1969.
- He received the death penalty in California, but after it was abolished he now serves a life term in that state.

# Donald Harvey
## (a.k.a. The Angel of Death)
## Ohio, 1952–

Facts:

- Killed at least 24 patients under his care at Drake Memorial Hospital in Cincinnati, OH in the 1980's.
- He had a very select target—the sick and dying in his hospital.
- He would put poison, chemicals, or air into their IV's or injections after sedating them.
- Said he had no remorse, and called them "mercy killings".
- There have been several copycat killings since.

## Theodore (Ted) Bundy
### (a.k.a. Chris Hagen)
### U.S. 1947–1989)

Facts:

- Accused of killing as many as 40 young, attractive women mostly in the western U.S. in the 1970's.
- He was a handsome, well educated, smooth-talker with a good sense of humor and was considered very trustworthy.
- One of his "tricks" was to fake an injury (like an arm in a sling) and then get women's attention by asking for their help.
- His earlier education made him very knowledgeable of the legal system.
- The evidence, that finally convicted him, was obtained when a wax impression of his teeth was secured (something he fought desperately not to give). It was a perfect match to the bite marks on one of the victim's buttocks.
- During the trial, he tried to convince the jury that he deserved a future because of what he had to offer the world.
- In the end he became quite a celebrity with his appeals to children to (1) stay in school, (2) follow the straight and narrow, and (3) to avoid using pornography.
- He got the electric chair on Jan. 24, 1989.

# David Berkowitz
## (a.k.a. Son of Sam)
## New York 1953–

Facts:

- He was born a bastard son of a woman who immediately gave him up for adoption.
- Knowing about the circumstances of his adoption he developed a deep sense of rejection and became very shy and horrified of women.
- Became deeply paranoid of people who he thought hated him (esp. women), which would keep him awake at nights.
- His murdering spree continued in the New York City area for 2 years and nearly paralyzed the entire city.
- In letters to the police he would use the word "wemen" instead of women—trying to belittle the sex.
- Some say he emulated Jack the Ripper.
- The name "Son of Sam" came from the name of his neighbor (Sam Carr) who owned a dog that kept him awake at nights. Berkowitz shot the dog (that survived) and from that point on claimed the dog spoke to him through one of his "voices" telling him to commit murder.
- He was sentenced to 365 years in prison with no chance of parole.

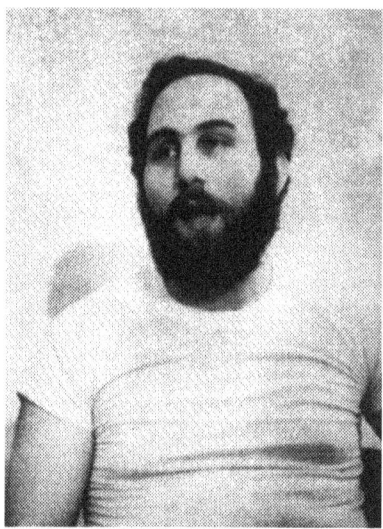

## Kenneth Bianchi and Angelo Buono
### (a.k.a. The Hillside Stranglers)
### California, Late 1970's

Facts:

- They were directly associated with at least 9 murders in less than 18 months.
- The series of murders were marked by kidnapping, rape, brutal torture, and then strangulation.
- Bodies were always disposed of nude, in obscene poses along the Los Angeles hillsides.
- Bianchi tried for an insanity plea, claiming he had Multiple Personality Disorder (MPD/DID) and it was one of his alter personalities that committed the murders.
- Both were sentenced to Life (without parole).

# Ted Kaczynski
## (a.k.a. The Unabomber)
## U.S., 1942–

Facts:

- Was described as a lonely, secretive, and obsessed man during his 25-year long (self-imposed) exile.

- At one time was one of the nation's top mathematicians with a degree from Harvard.

- Eventually became a recluse who shunned family and friends. His family described him as "a sad and tortured man".

- He started an 18-year long run of bombings that killed 3 and injured 29.

- The hunt for him became the FBI's most expensive they have ever had for a serial killer.

- He was also described as a cold, calculating, evil man with contempt for technological advancements.

- He is currently serving several life sentences in a Colorado prison where he remains silent about his crimes.

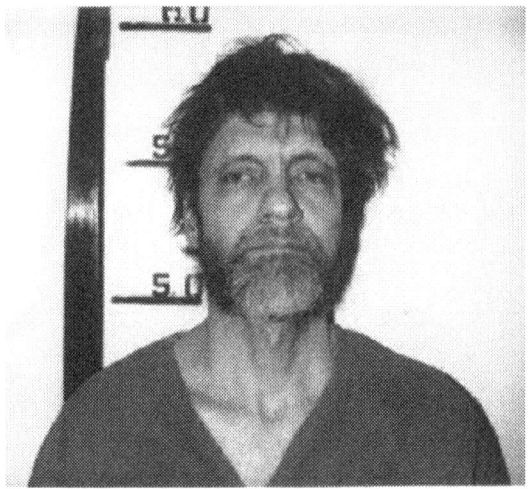

## Richard Ramirez
### (a.k.a. The Night Stalker)
### Los Angeles, CA 1953–

Facts:

- Was called "a living nightmare", a "bogey man" who invaded bedrooms in the middle of the night.

- A serial killer and rapist that was convicted on 43 counts, including 13 murders.

- He always attacked at night, sneaking into the victim's bedroom. The men were usually killed first with a quick bullet to the head. Females were kept alive to be victimized later after he ransacked the house looking for valuables. After raping and degrading the women, sometimes repeatedly, he would most often kill them.

- He was recently married (in San Quentin prison) where he is serving multiple life sentences.

# John Wayne Gacy
## (a.k.a. Patches or Pogo the Clown)
## Illinois, 1942–1994

Facts:

- His father was an alcoholic who beat him and his mother constantly.
- A habitual liar, Gacy was 5'8" and weighed well over 200 pounds. He was a man of only average intelligence.
- Convicted of killing at least 33 boys and young men.
- He often worked at children's parties where he performed as a clown.
- He would utilize his "handcuff trick" and "rope trick" to capture his victims.
- After reading the bible to them he would torture then kill them. After which he would bury them in a crawl space under his home near Chicago, IL.
- He was executed on May 10, 1994 where a large, and enthusiastic crowd cheered outside the Menard Correctional Center near Chester, IL.

## Jeffrey Dahmer
### Ohio and Milwaukee, WI 1960–1994

Facts:

- Led a somewhat normal life in Ohio until his family separated.

- He had unusual interests as a boy. He would collect dead insects and animals as well as pictures of internal body organs he could find from books and magazines.

- His pattern of crime would usually try to meet a young gay man, get him drunk or drug him, then kill him and have sex with him (the order of this last one depended on the willingness of the victim...).

- Some of the other perverse activities would include:
    + Taking the flesh and spicing it up to be eaten
    + Dismember and skin them (usually keeping the skulls)
    + On some victims he would drill holes in their head, then pore in acid which would turn them into zombies.

- He was found to be sane in the killing of 17 young men (16 in Wisconsin and 1 in Ohio).

- A fellow inmate killed Dahmer in 1994 at the Columbia Correctional Institution (Portage, WI).

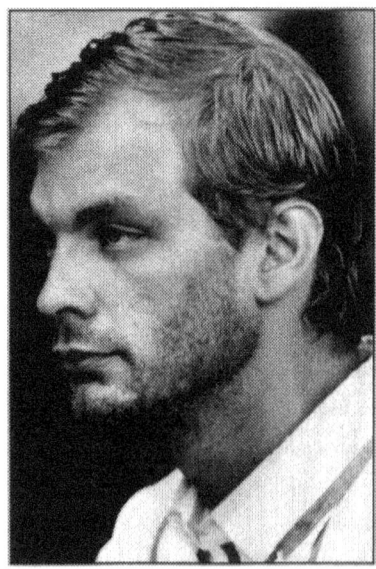

# Wayne Williams
## (a.k.a. The Atlanta Child Killer)
### Atlanta, GA 1958–

Facts:

- Involved in a 2-year reign of terror in the Atlanta area.
- Blamed for 23 to 30 homicides but was only convicted of 2 adult murders in 1982.
- Most of the believed child murders were by suffocation, asphyxiation, and strangulation. Some were stabbed.
- Called "a violent homosexual, bigot" that was so disgusted with his race that he hoped to wipe out future generations by killing black children before they could breed.
- Was finally caught when the famous "splash" was heard by an on-duty police rookie stationed on the Chattahoochee River, as Williams dumped the 21-year old Nathaniel Carter off a bridge.
- Now serving 2 life prison terms for the two adult killings.
- Most law enforcement personnel believe the 23-30 unsolved child murders were also solved with his arrest.

# Gary Ridgway
## (a.k.a. The Green River Killer)
### Seattle, WA 1949–

Facts:

- Confessed to 48 murders in Seattle's King County, WA (more murders than any other American serial killer).
- Began in 1982 and continued over a 19-month period.
- Raised in a fairly stable home, but the mother dominated the household—and especially Gary.
- People called him "friendly but strange".
- Seemed to be obsessed with prostitutes and had dysfunctional relationships with women.
- Said he hated prostitutes and killed so many he couldn't even remember. Most were dumped into the Green River.
- Caught by the 2 detectives involved in the capture of Ted Bundy.
- Convicting evidence was a saliva sample taken years ago that matched the DNA from a former crime scene.
- Serving 47 life sentences with no possibility of parole.

## Dennis Rader
### (a.k.a. The BTK Killer and Bill Thomas Killman)
### Wichita, KA 1945–

Facts:

-   Murdered at least 10 people in the Sedgwick County, KN area between 1974 and 1991.
-   When giving his calm and cold account of the killings he used such personal terms as:
    "Hit Kit"—His killing equipment
    "Projects"—His described crimes
    "Put them down"—Term for his murders
-   Surprised many when captured because he was a City Inspector, a Cub Scout Leader, and Lutheran Church council president.
-   Neighbors said he was "sometimes overzealous and extremely strict".
-   Police got a DNA sample from his daughter Kerri and matched it to her father's DNA that was taken from under the fingernails of a victim.
-   To this date has not apologized for any of the crimes. Trial has not begun at the time of this writing.

# Unit VII

## Social Psychology

# Chapter 18

## Psychology of Small Groups

*Small Group*—A gathering or unit of individuals who have face-to-face communication with one another, have a feeling of belonging to the group, and share a common goal.

*Influence of Small Groups*:

- Dyad: The smallest of groups (2 people), but often the most common.

- Distance between people: Can be a factor on how we interact considering whether or not you know the other person, if they approach you or you approach them, and if they are the same sex.

- Objects between people: How we put up protective barriers in our dealings with others.

- Size and Make-up of the group: Usually the larger the group, the less contact and communication—while smaller groups usually allows for more interaction. Also, if the group is all male, all female, or a mix can influence how we interact as well.

*Kinds of Groups:*

- Task-oriented Group: A group whose main purpose is to perform a specific job or task.

- Interaction-oriented Group: A group whose main purpose is to provide opportunity for social contacts or interaction.

- Inclusive Group: A group whose members get satisfaction from increasing their activity and trying to include more people.

- Exclusive Group: A group whose members get satisfaction from a feeling of being important.

- Informal Group: A group that is casual with no official structure.

- Formal Group: A group formed deliberately and with a rigid structure.

*Effects and interactions within Small Groups:*

- Size (2, 3, 4, 5*, even or odd numbers)

- To increase efficiency of the group:

  1. Control the discussion
  2. Prepare an agenda (*example on next page…)

**(Name of Agency)**
**Board Meeting Agenda**
(Month Day, Year)
(Location)
(Planned Starting Time to Ending Time)

| Activity | Action |
|---|---|
| Minutes from previous meeting | Approval |
| Chief Executive's Report | Discussion |
| Finance Committee's Report | Approve Budget Changes |
| Development Committee's Report *(nonprofit)* | Approve Fundraising Plan |
| Board Development Committee | Approve Plans for Retreat Adopt Resolution to Change ByLaws |

Other Business
- Old
- New
- Announcements
Roundtable Evaluation of Meeting
Review of Actions from Meeting
Adjourn

3.   Have materials/equipment on-hand and ready
4.   Type of seating
5.   Set a time limit
6.   Advantage/Disadvantage of taking breaks
7.   When to switch leaders

*Why people like to belong to Small Groups*:

-   Pleasure from the activities
-   A feeling of security
-   Gaining status
-   Business opportunities

*Attitudes within the Small Groups:*

- <u>Group Cohesiveness</u>: The mutual, overall attraction that each member feels toward others in the group.

- <u>Group Morale</u>: Attitudes of the individuals in a group, their loyalty to the group, and willingness to do the group's work.

- <u>Group Atmosphere</u>: The general emotional state of the group at any given time.

- <u>Group Climate</u>: The atmosphere that remains in a group over a long period of time.

*These attitudes are measurable through <u>Sociometry</u> (research on feelings of people in the groups, and by a <u>Sociogram</u> (diagram or chart that gives a visual view of the data). *Examples below…

SOCIOMETRY is the measurement of social distance between group members. More precisely, it is the assessment of attractions and repulsions between individuals in a group and with the group structure as defined by feelings. The method was first established by the social psychologist J.L. Moreno in 1934, and to this day, always involves a graphical depiction of the structure of group relations called a *sociogram*. The procedure for constructing a sociogram begins with a questionnaire-based sociometric test which asks each group member the following:

- name two or three peers you like the most, like working with, or are your best friends
- name two or three peers you least like, dislike working with, or that you reject as friends
- rate every member of the group in terms of like or dislike on a 5-point scale

After the mean ratings are collated, and one has identified what social structures exist, the researcher then locates appropriate guides, informants, and gatekeepers to the group. Fieldwork, or ethnography, is engaged in to obtain field notes. Together with a coding and analysis of one's field notes and the collated results of sociometric testing, the researcher draws up a sociogram depicting star and satellite cliques, dyads, triads, and so forth. The arrows in the sociogram contain a number obtained by dividing an individual's column score by n-1. A summary table usually accompanies the sociogram showing the frequency distributions. An example of a sociogram appears below:

*Roles in a Group*:

- Function (positions held or work to be done)
- Expected behavior based on personality (contributions to the group)
- Age (the influence of young vs. old)

*Communication within a Group*: Passing on of information from one individual to another (e.g. verbal and nonverbal).

- *Group Feedback*: Gaining an idea of how well or how poorly the group is doing.

- Pseudogroup Effect: The incorrect assumption that certain results are due to your group influence.

# Chapter 19

## Social Influence

*Attitude*—A readiness to respond favorably or unfavorably to a person, object, situation, or event. Once these attitudes are formed they tend not to change too much.

*Social Attitude*—Attitudes that relate to social situations, problems, and questions.

*Prejudice*—An attitude that prevents us from objectively considering and evaluating new evidence.

**Setting an Example**
Raising our children and understanding racial diversity in our society can't be seen as separate tasks—they're both part of our job.

*Propaganda*—Any organized attempt to influence social attitudes.

**Types of Propaganda**
There are many techniques commonly used in the dissemination of propaganda.

**BANDWAGON:** The basic idea behind the bandwagon approach is just that, "getting on the bandwagon." The propagandist puts forth the idea that everyone is doing this, or everyone supports this person/cause, so should you. The bandwagon approach appeals to the conformist in all of us: No one wants to be left out of what is perceived to be a popular trend.

**EXAMPLE:** Everyone in Lemmingtown is behind Jim Duffie for Mayor. Shouldn't you be part of this winning team?

**TESTIMONIAL:** This is the celebrity endorsement of a philosophy, movement or candidate. In advertising, for example, athletes are often paid millions of dollars to promote sports shoes, equipment and fast food. In political circles, movie stars, television stars, rock stars and athletes lend a great deal of credibility and power to a political cause or candidate. Just a photograph of a movie star at political rally can generate more interest in that issue/candidate or cause thousands, sometimes millions, of people to become supporters.

**EXAMPLE:** "Sam Slugger", a baseball Hall of Famer who led the pros in hitting for years, appears in a television ad supporting Mike Politico for U.S. Senate. Since Sam is well known and respected in his home state and nationally, he will likely gain Mr. Politico many votes just by his appearance with the candidate.

**PLAIN FOLKS:** Here the candidate or cause is identified with common people from everyday walks of life. The idea is to make the candidate/cause come off as grassroots and all-American.
**EXAMPLE:** After a morning speech to wealthy Democratic donors, Bill Clinton stops by McDonald's for a burger, fries, and photo-op.

**TRANSFER:** Transfer employs the use of symbols, quotes or the images of famous people to convey a message not necessarily associated with them. In the use of transfer, the candidate/speaker attempts to persuade us through the indirect use of something we respect, such as a patriotic or religious image, to promote his/her ideas. Religious and patriotic images may be the most commonly used in this propaganda technique but they are not alone. Sometimes even science becomes the means to transfer the message.

**EXAMPLE:** The environmentalist group people promoting plants, in its attempt to prevent a highway from destroying the natural habitat of thousands of plant species, produces a television ad with a "scientist" in a white lab coat explaining the dramatic consequences of altering the food chain by destroying this habitat.

**FEAR:** This technique is very popular among political parties and PACs (Political Action Committees) in the U.S. The idea is to present a dreaded circumstance and usually follow it up with the kind of behavior needed to avoid that horrible event.

**EXAMPLE:** The Citizens for Retired Rights present a magazine ad showing an elderly couple living in poverty because their social security benefits have been drastically cut by the Republicans in Congress. The solution? The CRR urges you to vote for Democrats.

**LOGICAL FALLACIES:** Applying logic, one can usually draw a conclusion from one or more established premises. In the type of propaganda known as the logical fallacy, however, the premises may be accurate but the conclusion is not.

**EXAMPLE:**

- Premise 1: Bill Clinton supports gun control.

- Premise 2: Communist regimes have always supported gun control.

- Conclusion: Bill Clinton is a communist.

We can see in this example that the Conclusion is created by a twisting of logic, and is therefore a fallacy.

**GLITTERING GENERALITIES:** This approach is closely related to what is happening in TRANSFER (see above). Here, a generally accepted virtue is usually employed to stir up favorable emotions. The problem is that these words mean different things to different people and are often manipulated for the propagandists' use. The important thing to remember is that in this technique the propagandist uses these words in a positive sense. They often include words like: democracy, family values (when used positively), rights, civilization, even the word "American."

**EXAMPLE:** An ad by a cigarette manufacturer proclaims to smokers: Don't let them take your rights away! ("Rights" is a powerful word, something that stirs the emotions of many, but few on either side would agree on exactly what the 'rights' of smokers are.)

**NAME-CALLING:** This is the opposite of the glittering generalities approach. Name-calling ties a person or cause to a largely perceived negative image.

**EXAMPLE:** In a campaign speech to a logging company, the Congressman referred to his environmentally conscious opponent as a "tree hugger."

*Cognitive Dissonance*—When individuals are faced with a lack of agreement between ideas, attitudes, or beliefs.

*Attribution*—A process by which we attempt to interpret and explain the behavior of others.

- Dispositional Factor: Where behavior is attributed to the personality of the individual.
- Situational Factor: Where the behavior is attributed to the situation or environment.

**Leadership**—A leader is an individual who exerts great influence on a group. They suggest, organize, and direct the activities of the group. They help to guide the thinking of the group, and inspire members to establish and work toward goals. Authority vs. Responsibility. Psychologists would suggest that leaders are not born—they are made.

*Kinds of Leaders*:

- Those who "get the job done" and solve the problems
- The "charismatic" leaders that lead through their popularity and personality.

*Personalities of Leaders*:

- Intellectual (respected wisdom, experience, and intelligence)
- Well Adjusted (ability to change and understand)

- Outgoing (friendly, communicative, and extroverted)
- Dominating (Aggressive and in control)
- Understanding (willing to listen to others)
- Sensitive to Interpersonal Relationships (considerate of personalities and relations within the group)

*Techniques or Styles of Leadership:*

- Democratic Leader: Works "with" their group by welcoming contributions and suggestions.

- Autocratic Leader: Directs the operation of their group with a firm hand.

- Laissez-faire Leader: A passive style of leadership that will step-in or assists when asked or needed.

*Peers*—Persons considered to be our equals, usually of the same age and ability.

*Role Models*—Persons who provide examples of behavior that others might want to copy.

*Phrases and Concepts of Peer Interaction:*

- Risky Shift: A group or individual will take more chances than they would if by themselves.
- Autokenetic Illusion (or Effect): Experiment to show peer influence.

*Roles*—The kind of behavior that is expected of us in a social situation.

*Male and Female Roles:*

- Culture: How society views the actions of males and females
- Biological: The physical differences of the sexes
- Parent Teaching: How we are influenced in early childhood

- <u>Media</u>: How TV, Radio, and Print media influence how we behave
- <u>Other</u>: Family roles, titles, and wartime participation

# Chapter 20

## Social Interaction

**Helping Others:**

*Altruistic Behavior*—The act of offering to help or giving help to other people

Reasons why we might be inclined to help others:

- Influence of your mood
- Physical attractiveness of the individual
- Health or Age status of the individual
- Helping would make you feel good

*Diffusion of Responsibility*—People in a group do not feel as responsible for offering aid as when they are alone. The attitude of "passing on" the responsibility.

*Social Facilitation*—When individuals do better in a group situation than when they work alone.

- Among animals (ant farms, bee hives, migratory birds, etc.)
- Among humans (studying, rivalries and competitions, etc.)

*Social Competition*—When people do better in social situations when there are rivalries and competition involved.

Examples of behaviors in Social Competition:

- "Pecking Order" (the hierarchy of dominance or authority)
- "Use of a Threat" (as a motivational technique)
- "Playing Chicken" (who will be the first to back down)
- Social, Occupational, and Recreational
- Within Minority Groups (as a means to succeed)
- Between Nations (land, history, wealth, etc.)

*The Effects of Competition*:

- Can create confusion and inefficiency
- Some will try to win at any price
- The many negative effects of losing
- "Hostile Aggression"—Responding to a situation in ways that are intentionally harmful to others and not for purposes of self-defense.

*Social Cooperation*:

- In Animals (warmth, food, cleaning, etc.)
- In Humans (profit-sharing, neighborhood watches, etc.)
- Hopi Indian Tribe (consider helping another as the highest of virtues)
- Need for communication (the more information shared within the community increases the chances for mutual cooperation)

# Appendix D

## Sport Psychology
## (A study of Athletes, Coaches, and Parents)

**Winning:**

Is your definition: (1) Finish 1$^{st}$, ahead of the rest of the competition OR (2) Giving your best effort during the competition.

**Three Keys To Success:**

1.  **Commitment** (Measure of how dedicated the athlete is to training toward an athletic goal)

    -   Individual desire
    -   Personal sacrifice
    -   How much is too much, or not enough?

2.  **Communication** (How you speak or act toward...)

    -   Your Coach
    -   Other Athletes
    -   From Within Yourself

3.  **Attitude** (Individual emotions, feelings, thoughts, and actions toward competition)

- Positive attitude (showing your joy)
- Negative attitude (shying away, poor effort, frustration, etc.)

**The "Mental Game":** (should be an equal balance, physical & mental…)

1. Identify the challenge ahead
2. Assess the difficulty of the challenge
3. Prepare to cope with, manage, and meet the challenges

## "The Climb to Success"

### Long Term Goals

### Short Term Goals (everyday goals)

## Mental Preparation:

- Make yourself mentally familiar with all aspects of the competition
- Try to "visualize" the scene of the competition (the field, the weather, the other competitors, etc.)

- Keep a Journal of:
    + Pre-event activities
    + How you did
    + How you felt before and after
- Materialistic Goals: Those you can actually measure (times, hits, etc.)
- Non-materialistic Goals: Any inner feelings of satisfaction

## Getting "Psyched Up":

- Motivation:
    + Extrinsic (rewards, fame, etc.)
    + Intrinsic (inner desires to succeed)

+    Combination (putting the 2 together)
-    "Inverted U Theory" (a bimodal theory)
    1.    Getting too emotional
    2.    Not getting emotional enough
- Methods of preparations for that solid competition
    +    listen to music, or motivational speeches
    +    eat a proper pre-competition meal
    +    get plenty of sleep the night before
    +    watch a motivating movie
    +    just relax with teammates
    +    watch tapes of previous competitions
    +    or any other method that makes you feel comfortable

**How to better Concentrate** (or improve your attention span…)

-    Direction (external or internal?) and Width (broad or narrow?)
-    "Blocking Out" (external noises, distractions, etc.)

Stress in Competition:

-    Good Aspects (adrenaline, muscle tension, focus…)
-    Bad Aspects (worry, loss of confidence, fine motor skills lost…)
-    Signs of feeling the stress:
    +    sweaty palms
    +    nervousness
    +    "butterflies"
-    Relaxation Techniques:
    +    muscle relaxation, meditation, deep breathing
    +    listening to your favorite music

**Burnout** (Trying too hard for unreachable goals, or overextending your body And mind)

- "Little League Syndrome" (caused by high expectations of parents)
- Working too hard to achieve unattainable goals
- Indicators of possible Burnout:
    + Too much dedication to training
    + Not feeling any joy in the competition
    + Too serious an attitude at practice
    + Too much drive to achieve success
- How to avoid Burnout:
    + Take some time off
    + Try other things (music, another sport, etc.)

**How to enjoy the game more…**

- Compete against your own potential
- Celebrate (respectfully) a personal victory
- As a coach, acknowledge a job well done

# References and Index to Authors

American Psychiatric Association, *Diagnostic and Statistical Manual of Mental Disorders* (IV and IV-TR Editions), 1995 and 2001.

Anderson, Barry F., *The Psychology Experiment*. Brooks/Cole Publishing, 1966.

Butter, Charles, M., *Neuropsychology: The Study of Brain Behavior*. Brooks/Cole, 1968.

*Bunker, M. N.,* Handwriting Analysis: The Science of Determining Personality By Graphoanalysis. *Nelson-Hall Co. Publishing, 1972.*

Conger, John J., *Adolescence and Youth*. Harper and Row Publishers, 1973.

Crisp, Tony. Dream Dictionary. Wings Books, 1990.

Engle, T.L. and Snellgrove, Louis. *Psychology: Its Principles and Applications*.

Harcourt, Brace, Jovanich Publications, 1989.

Google Images. (www.google.com) *Graphics

Janis, Irving L.; Mahl, George F.; Kagan, Jerome, and Holt; Robert R. *Personality: Dynamics, Development, and Assessment*. Harcourt, Brace and World, Inc., 1969.

Luftman, Susan., Sports Psychology. Human Relations Media, 1990.

McGinnies, Elliott. *Social Behavior: A Functional Analysis*. Houghton Mifflin *Co., Boston. 1970*

Millett, Kate. *Sexual Politics*. Doubleday and Co., 1970.

Nextext. *Introduction to Psychology*. Houghton Mifflin Co., 2001.

Rathus, Spencer A. *Psychology: Principles in Practice*. Holt, Rinehart and Winston, 1998.

Restak, Richard M., M.D. *The Mind*. Bantam Books. 1988.

Rickman, John M.D. *A General Selection From The Works Of Sigmund Freud*. Anchor Books (Doubleday), 1989.

Wikipedia: The Free Encyclopedia (www.wikipedia.com) *Violent Minds biographies and images.

# About The Author

This attractive man of genius has chosen to give up his summer pursuit to become the starting shortstop for the New York Yankees long enough to create this book. Once romantically linked to the actress Catherine Zeta-Jones (despite rumors of the current restraining order), he now lives a quiet existence in the metropolis known as Medford, Wisconsin. Although only in his late 20's (very late maybe) he has the look of an experienced writer in his early 70's. Although not a Psychologist, he did stay in a Holiday Inn Express last night.

978-0-595-36869-3
0-595-36869-7

www.ingramcontent.com/pod-product-compliance
Lightning Source LLC
Chambersburg PA
CBHW022247290526
45785CB00015B/389